THE 1926 ORLAND PARK MURDER MYSTERY

MATTHEW T. GALIK

THE History PRESS

Published by The History Press
Charleston, SC
www.historypress.com

Front cover, top, and back cover, bottom: courtesy of Richard Quinn.
Front cover, bottom: National Archives.

First published 2018

Manufactured in the United States

ISBN 9781467139915

Library of Congress Control Number: 2018945792

Notice: The information in this book is true and complete to the best of our knowledge. It is offered without guarantee on the part of the author or The History Press. The author and The History Press disclaim all liability in connection with the use of this book.

For Ethel, Lucille and Rosalyn Fisher,
Barney Hostert, Dr. Ernest McMahan
and all others whose lives were changed by the events of April 14, 1926

CONTENTS

ACKNOWLEDGEMENTS

In spending close to fifteen years researching the narrative that has built this volume, I have had the pleasure to cross paths with many skilled historians, dedicated researchers and dear friends who have in some way directly helped me connect dots, brush the dust from long-forgotten incidents, bring the past to life and think outside the box. In no particular order, I'd like to thank longtime village educator and former Mokena mayor Richard Quinn, who from an early date provided great interest not only in the case detailed herein but also in the project of writing this book itself. I also could never forget Carol Tracy of the Mokena Public Library, an informational wizard for whom no question is too obscure. She has known me since I was knee high to a grasshopper. I'd be remiss not to remember master genealogist Tina Beaird of the Plainfield Public Library, who always reminds me to check the hidden nooks and crannies of the past, most of which I never would have thought of otherwise. I greatly appreciate the work of Doug Williford of the National Archives at San Francisco, who put me on the path of a vital paper trail. I'd like to thank my parents, who have selflessly provided input in countless areas in this project. My hat goes off to Dave Kropp, who is not only a great conversation partner and a true Mokenian but one of my dearest friends. While no longer among us, I must remember Chuck Hostert, another Mokenian who not only was part of a great local family but also was a nice guy who told me some pretty amazing stories. It was a joy speaking with Dottie Ferrentino, who I had the pleasure to get to know only briefly before she left us. She made her stepfather, who I previously had only known from faded newsprint, a living being in a way no one else could.

INTRODUCTION

The night of April 14, 1926, found Al Hruby tending to business at the Airdrome Tavern in Broadview, Illinois. The village was a quiet one, located twelve miles west of Chicago's Loop, and until a few years prior had been known for being the Windy City's airmail hub. Hruby owned his place; in the following days, he would call it a restaurant, while the press would come to derisively refer to it as a roadhouse, which, according to the jargon of the era, meant that illegal booze could have secretly flowed there. With the daily comings and goings likely winding down that Wednesday evening, Hruby was surprised to see a man and two women who had just left his place come bursting back through the Airdrome's doors around 11:15 p.m.

Theirs was frantic, jumbled talk of something in the middle of Twenty-Second Street, just a short distance down the road and to the east. Was it a body? Al Hruby would later state that his first instinct was that the man was the victim of an accident, perhaps brought on by illegal, rotgut alcohol that could be easily had in and around Chicago. Hruby soon found himself driving down Twenty-Second Street with two buddies, trailing behind the people who had let him know. As the brightness of the auto's headlights cut a swath through the inky April darkness, their car slowed when Hruby caught something in their glow—something out of the ordinary.

The auto idled, and Hruby emerged to get a closer look at the figure sprawled in this desolate stretch of road. His eyes were filled with the unforgettable sight of carnage; this was much more serious than a bad hangover. With the hum of his car droning behind him, Hruby saw the crimson streak of a bloody tire print leading away from the man. As his eyes slowly came into focus, he recognized that the man before him was motionless and gory, his body punctured with bullet holes.

In time, the swarthy, neatly dressed man discovered in Twenty-Second Street by Hruby and his customers would prove to be a corpse. To investigators, it was business as usual, just another one of the 729 unsolved murders that occurred in and around Chicago during the Prohibition era. Images of pearl-bedecked flappers doing the Charleston, the great silent film stars Harold Lloyd and Colleen Moore and the burgeoning Art Deco style fill our minds with the mention of the Roaring Twenties. To the majority of us in the early twenty-first century, the events of this decade are far removed yet still clear in our collective psyche. It was a decade of excess and heady exuberance, one in which the United States' victory in World War I was still fresh, the American economy expanded at a dizzying rate and exciting new technology such as the radio, automobile and airplane flourished.

The Jazz Age also was an era that bred a wave of crime and bloodshed, particularly in and around Chicago. Having faced increased pressure from the strong anti-liquor lobby, the federal government's passage of the Volstead Act in 1919 led to previously unheard-of levels of crime. Despite the nationwide prohibition of the manufacturing and selling of alcoholic beverages, speakeasies could be found in nearly every American city of consequence. Brutal gang wars between rival factions of bootleggers were commonplace, especially in Chicago, which in the particularly bloody year of 1924 was thrust into the "Bootleg Battle of the Marne."

Al Hruby's grisly discovery of Santo Calabrese's corpse on that April evening in 1926 was the link to two now long-forgotten crimes that shook the Chicago region. A multi-thousand-dollar mail heist and the subsequent brutal shooting of a Will County sheriff's deputy the same day would, in time, come to be woven together as one by law enforcement and the media. The events would shape the fates of three men of diverse backgrounds and change the lives of all those involved, although to this day, many questions surrounding them remain unanswered.

CHAPTER 1

THE HEART OF A COMMUNITY

As every story has its end, every tale also has a beginning. Ours takes us to the sleepy, rural village of Mokena, Illinois. Comprising the northern half of Frankfort Township in eastern Will County, Mokena and the surrounding region were composed mostly of hearty second- and third-generation German Americans who gained their livelihoods through the fertile earth or the herds of dairy cows that grazed the land. The residents of Mokena proper lived here and there in modern bungalows but mostly in simple nineteenth-century wood-frame houses whose walls occasionally could be found caked in soot from passing locomotives. Wolf Road, a dirt path that led to and from the village, became impassable in anything less than perfect weather. The number of Mokena's inhabitants hovered around 475 for the first half of the 1920s, up more than twofold from the turn of the twentieth century.

Although Mokena was a country village, it didn't lack for fun. Various social groups organized by the four town churches (three Protestant and one Catholic) entertained area youth, as did the vastness of the surrounding countryside, with woods ideal for hunting and placid Hickory Creek perfect for fishing. A large, wooden dance pavilion located in the shade of Cappel's Grove off Wolf Road drew crowds from miles around. Joliet, the hub of Will County, with its new Rialto Theater and myriad stores and restaurants, was but a short trip west down the Chicago, Rock Island and Pacific Railroad.

The only industry to be spoken of in Mokena was a milk bottling plant run by the Bowman Dairy Company of Chicago. Due to a recent dispute between

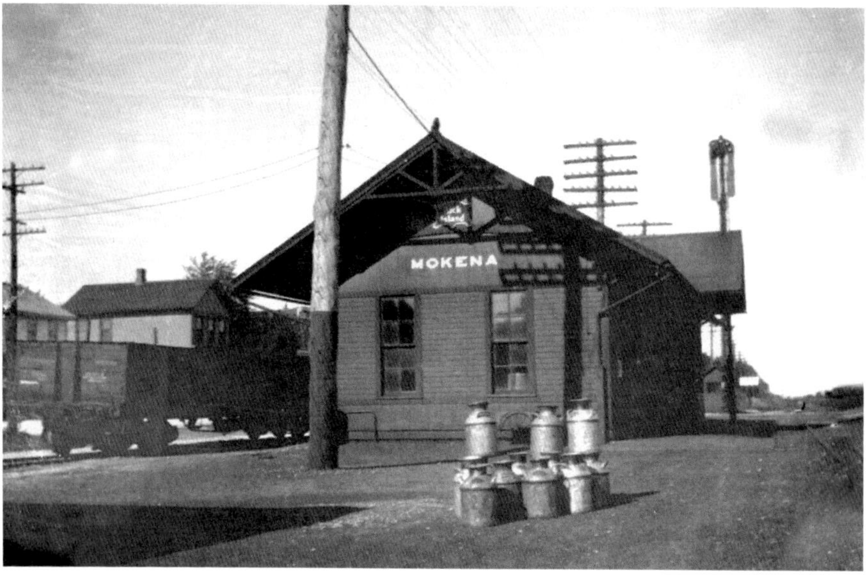

An old landmark in town, the Chicago, Rock Island and Pacific Railroad depot at Mokena, is seen in this circa 1920 view. *Courtesy Richard Quinn.*

health authorities and area farmers regarding cattle vaccinations, the plant was shuttered by the company in 1926. Houses of business lined Front Street in 1926 as they had for decades in Mokena's past. A large, rambling building housed the blacksmith shop of Al Braun, where the sparks flew on a daily basis. The small yet respected Mokena State Bank stood proudly with a colonnaded façade of Bedford stone, and the pharmacy of Richard Hensel dispensed not only medicine but also sweet treats from its soda fountain. Iron goods were supplied by Milton and Roy Krapp, proprietors of the Mokena Hardware Company. Automotive needs were seen to by Elmer Cooper and Barney Hostert in their large and centrally located garage, which in turn also served as a kind of informal city hall, a place where Mokena's men would gather to "cuss and discuss" issues of the day.

Current events were recorded in a small yet lively newspaper called the *News-Bulletin.* Editor William Semmler published the paper from a historic Front Street building, passionately boosting Mokena and promoting local thought. A prime example of reportage from the young newsman's publication would be the story of "wreaths of smoke" discovered emanating from an abandoned Front Street structure by the local fire marshal. Upon quick investigation, it was found that "a gang of boys had used the cellar for a dugout. Straw, papers, oil and gasoline were found." With stern

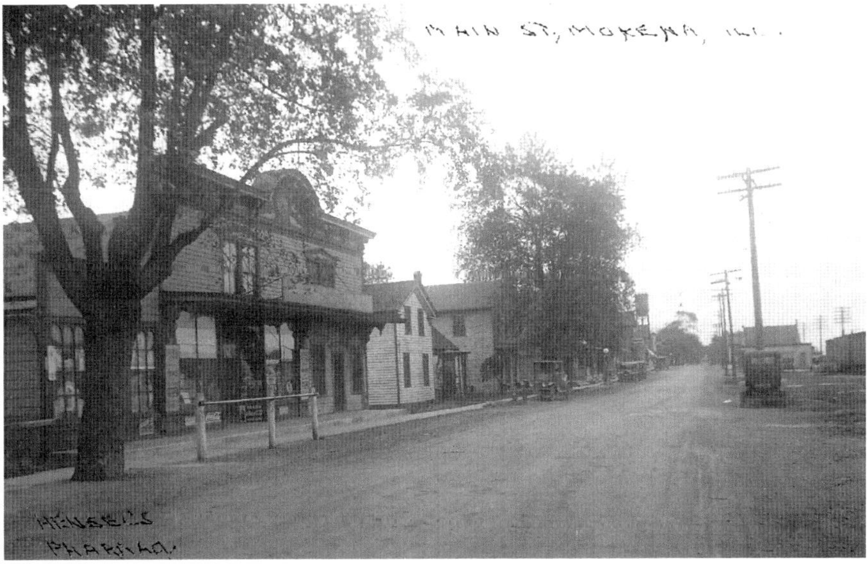

The picturesque Hensel Pharmacy is seen around 1925 in this eastward-facing postcard of Mokena's Front Street. *Courtesy Richard Quinn.*

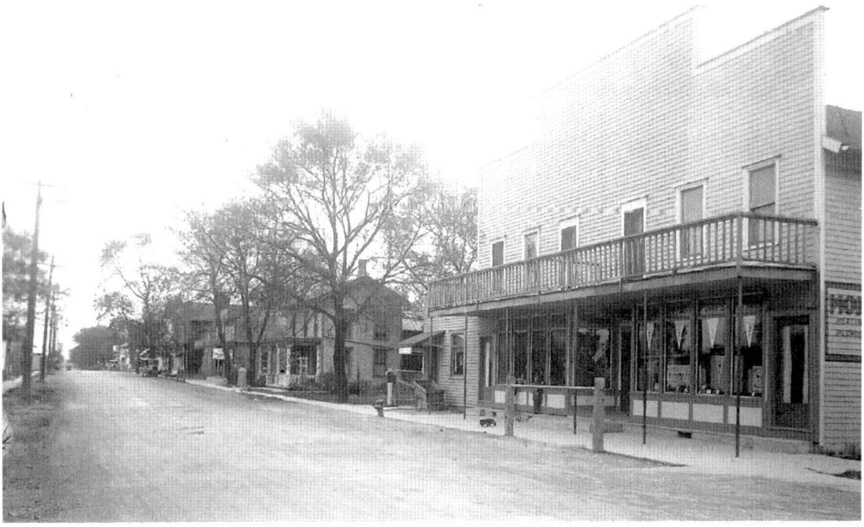

Situated on the northwest corner of Front and Division Streets in Mokena, the Mokena Hardware Company is pictured here circa 1925. *Courtesy Richard Quinn.*

admonition not to repeat the practice, the boys were turned loose by the marshal to face their parents.

Beneath the bucolic exterior of Mokena life in the 1920s, a darker, more sinister side lurked. The crime wave experienced since the passage of the 1919 Volstead Act found its way to Mokena, having emerged from the murky depths like filthy tentacles. Not thirty-five miles to the north, the Thompson submachine gun was earning in blood its moniker, "the Chicago Typewriter." Fifteen miles as the crow flew east, Chicago Heights was a nest of activity for bootleggers affiliated with the gang of Chicago's John Torrio. In Joliet, the seat of Will County, eleven miles due west of Mokena, notorious Chicago bootlegger Spike O'Donnell[1] kept two illegal breweries functioning, where the Lipsey brothers also held their bootlegger's court.

The pages of editor Semmler's *News-Bulletin* have left a stirring record of the times, an era filled with lawbreaking and intrigue. Some of the first instances to mark the arrival of this new era were the presence of strange men in town, individuals who were known to no one and carried an ominous air about themselves. In the summer of 1921, one man, described as a "foreigner" (usually a term denoting Mediterranean descent), was noticed purchasing large quantities of raisins from a Mokena store. The transaction was noted to "raise the question if a moonshine still is in operation." On another occasion, two strangers turned up at the Illinois Bell Telephone office on Front Street and asked many unsettling questions. Their curiosity was piqued in regard to the conditions in the small local jail and the strength of the local police. Having the appearance of men who were under the influence, they attempted to place several long-distance calls and left some mysterious, heavy suitcases at the office before disappearing.[2]

The summer of 1924 saw the discovery of a brewery secreted in the dank wine cellars of an old farm near neighboring Frankfort, a find that shut down one of the biggest illegal booze operations in the state.[3] Shortly after Mokena's entry into 1925, Will County authorities raided a Mokena establishment belonging to George Wannemacher. Liquor and illegal gambling equipment were seized, confirming the suspicions of many in the village of nefarious activities at the place.[4] Wannemacher happened to serve as a trustee on the Mokena Village Board. Federal Prohibition agents were known to have visited the village on at least one occasion, having probed the railroad shipment of a boxcar's weight of beer in 1922.[5]

Nevertheless, far more evil crimes were afoot in 1920s Mokena than mere alcohol offenses. The village jail was sprayed with gunfire in the middle of a spring night in 1922 after two runaway boys were housed there.[6] The reason for the mysterious shooting was never discovered. Not long after, a group of four hoods from Joliet nearly murdered local farmer Henry Yunker while he attempted to pull their stalled auto from a muddy patch in front of his farm. With overblown bravado, the ruffians covered him with revolvers and a sawed-off shotgun while he nervously worked, simply to prove that they could.[7] In October 1923, two well-dressed robbers shot at the postmaster of neighboring Orland Park, then just called Orland, slightly wounding him during a brazen hold-up of his general store.[8] The following October, five bandits robbed the Mokena State Bank of over $4,000 in a daring daylight heist. Armed to the teeth, the thieves forced the bank president, who was also the mayor, to scoop stacks of cash from the safe into a gunny sack. Even though authorities managed to trace tire prints from the getaway car for miles over dirt roads, the criminals made a successful escape.[9] In a reflection of the era, Will County sheriff Newkirk suggested that each township deputize several men for the "arrest of moonshiners, bootleggers, and auto thieves."

Editor Semmler of the *News-Bulletin* took an early and decidedly anti-crime stance in his paper. By 1926, issues were appearing with a masthead that read "Square for Law Enforcement, Right, and Truth." In a front-page editorial referencing ground zero for the Capone Syndicate's activity, a reflective Semmler lamented that "it will only be a short time before Frankfort (Township) will be a second Cicero with gunmen and thugs." He ended the column with a warning to his readers to "wake up" and not "let the denizens of the underworld catch you sleeping!" A lack of modern highway police laws was a great benefit to the criminals of the place and era, who, in the August 1924 words of editor Semmler, "race up and down the state…robbing, plundering, and murdering at will." Thus, the stage was set. Like a shield protecting his townsfolk from the perils of his era, a key player in the events to follow was a young man named Walter Fisher.

CHAPTER 2

THE MOKENIAN WALTER FISHER

Before his name was made immortal by history, he was an ordinary man. The keeper of a respected general merchandise store in Mokena, Walter Fisher came from a place much different socially and politically from the one he would later call home. Born in the Russian Empire and of Jewish faith and heritage, his background set him apart from other townsfolk and made him unique. During the period in which Fisher lived and worked in the area, there was only one other man in Mokena known to come from the Judaic tradition: David Kolber, of Austro-Hungarian birth,[10] who conducted a hardware store at Front and Mokena Streets.

Walter Fisher's life dawned on October 25, 1897,[11] in the ancient Slavic city of Minsk. Having passed through the hands of Lithuanians and Poles over the course of its long existence, just before the start of the twentieth century, the city was one with the Russian Empire and Czar Nicholas II. The son of young Benjamin Fisher and his wife, Frieda, the surviving historic record indicates that Walter was the first child to have graced their union. The lot of the Fishers in their homeland would have undoubtedly been a hard one, a fate made no easier by their faith. The year of Walter's birth saw the Jewish population in Minsk number nearly fifty thousand, they and their families having over the span of centuries been the subject of oppression by any given ruler. As early as the seventeenth century, Jews were disallowed from conducting commerce within city limits, and while this right was later reinstated, ruthless pogroms and forced conversion to Christianity were not unheard of in Eastern Europe.

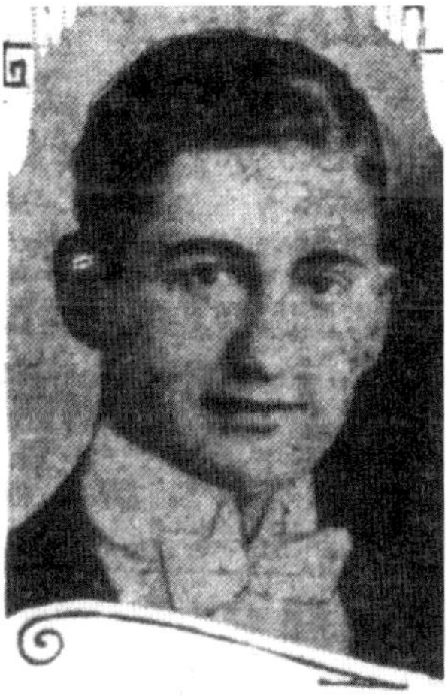

Published in the *Chicago American* in the aftermath of his death, this image of Walter Fisher is the only known to exist. *Author's collection.*

While no solid details of Walter Fisher's earliest years are known, the hardscrabble life that was the lot of the Russian Empire's Jews is what likely spurred his father, Benjamin Fisher, to flee tyranny and take up new residence in the United States. After Benjamin's journey across the ocean and securing of American home and hearth, Frieda and six-year-old Walter joined him. The family became one in their new home around 1903. The Fishers, who may have anglicized their names, were found by a federal census taker in Louisville, Kentucky, in 1910. There, Walter would have later recalled his father peddling dry goods[12] in the city's sizeable Jewish neighborhood, toiling the long, hard hours that characterized the immigrant's life in America. Such as it was for countless children in that era, young Fisher's formal education ended with grammar school.

Mindful of the slog of his parents to build a better life for him, Walter became a full-fledged American citizen by the time he was a young man. He also became the big brother to three siblings, all born in the United States. Ella and Max Fisher were born while the family still lived in Kentucky, and Esther entered this world after the Fishers moved north to Illinois. Walter grew to become a handsome man, with brown eyes and dark hair that swept tightly across his head. Stoutly built, he had a soft, almost cherubic smile. It's easy to see what Ethel Lewis saw in him, the girl being a year Walter's junior. As America was preparing to enter the bloody tumult of World War I, their young minds were focused on love, and Walter and Ethel were married on February 24, 1917, the union being sealed by Rabbi Joseph Itkin of Joliet's B'nei Jacob Congregation.[13]

The Lewises were Jews of Polish descent,[14] an ethnic group that had much in common with other European Jews in terms of eventual prosecution in their homeland. Ethel's father, Joe Lewis, kept a respected general store in Joliet, a city of industry and the seat of Will County, located about forty-five miles southwest of Chicago. Home of well-heeled Americans and new immigrants, Joliet was not foreign territory to Jews, as their first organized congregation in the city was formed in 1893, followed by a Hebrew school in 1911.[15] Within a year of his marriage, Walter went to work in his father-in-law's store and, with Ethel, would come to call a little place at 207 Meeker Avenue his home.

While in Joliet, the young couple was blessed by the birth of their first child in February 1918, a little daughter whom Walter and Ethel named Lucille. Another daughter, Rosalyn Joyce, was born on March 7, 1920. The county seat was not to become the Fishers' permanent home, however, for early in 1922 they relocated to Mokena, to which fate would forever bind them. Whether Mokena was a richer environment for business or a better place for their two small daughters, what drew the Fishers to the village eleven miles east of Joliet remains unclear. Upon his coming to Mokena, Walter bought Grogan's Kash and Karry, a small grocery store on the northwest corner of Front and Division Streets that was in the midst of going out of business.[16]

Walter Fisher was off to a brisk start in town, which at this time boasted a population of roughly 475. Aware of his status as newcomer in the small, rural village, he made a distinct effort to pierce the insular shell of his new

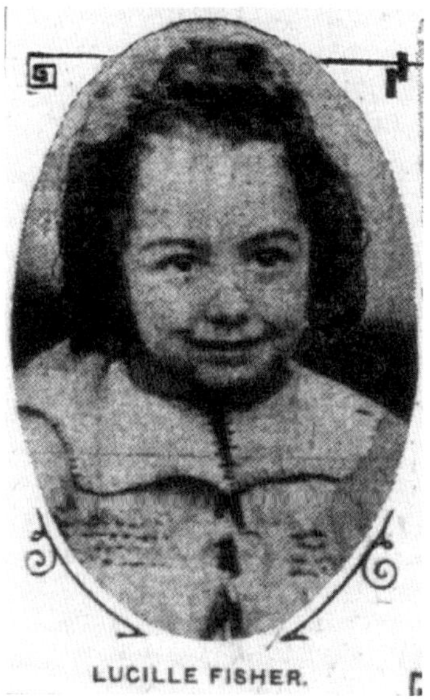

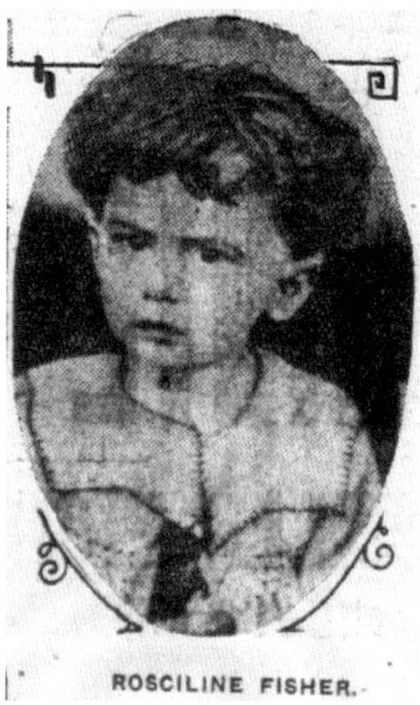

Left: Lucille Fisher was Walter and Ethel's eldest daughter, having entered the world in February 1918. *Author's collection.*

Right: Born in March 1920, Rosalyn Fisher was Walter and Ethel's second daughter. Her name was unfortunately misspelled when this photo appeared in the *Chicago American* in April 1926. *Author's collection.*

neighbors. Taking a step forward with his hand metaphorically outstretched in friendship, he posted an ad in the February 10, 1922 edition of the *News-Bulletin* under the heading "Meet Me at the Post-Office." Ever the businessman, he extolled his ability to help his customers save and introduced himself with the words "I will become a taxpayer and citizen of Mokena," adding that he would "have the pleasure of meeting everybody personally." The Mokenians warmed up to him from the start, and his venture with the grocery store paid off so well for Walter that he had to remodel the place to accommodate more shelves for his wares.[17] He soon expanded his line to include not only foodstuffs but also a vast variety of dry goods. In 1923, items to be had from Walter Fisher included men's and children's union suits, women's hosiery, mason jars and canned peas (two for twenty-five cents). High-end goods, such as a "complete line of phonographs," were advertised in the *News-Bulletin* starting at ninety-eight dollars, along with a variety of records at forty-nine cents each. If there were any questions, Walter would gladly demonstrate.[18]

Editor Semmler described Walter as a "live Mokena merchant" whose consistent advertising was paying off for him in big ways. After a certain notice had been placed in the village paper, Walter received a phone call from a costumer about nine miles distant, near the small Cook County village of Orland Park. The grocery order in question was a large one, filling half an auto, and was delivered by Fisher himself.[19] In the summer of 1922, while thinking of a way to sell cooking oil, Walter carried on a demonstration of it at the store on a Saturday evening, giving away the "fried cakes" to any customers who stopped by. The townsfolk of Mokena had been invited, Fisher having stated that "everyone is welcome."[20] The Fishers were getting along nicely in the village. Walter was part of the Modern Woodmen in Mokena, while Ethel came to be a member of the Royal Neighbors of America, both fraternal beneficiary societies.[21] During a brief period in 1922 when the village had no postmaster, Walter was appointed assistant postmaster and appears to have maintained the post office in a space within his store.[22]

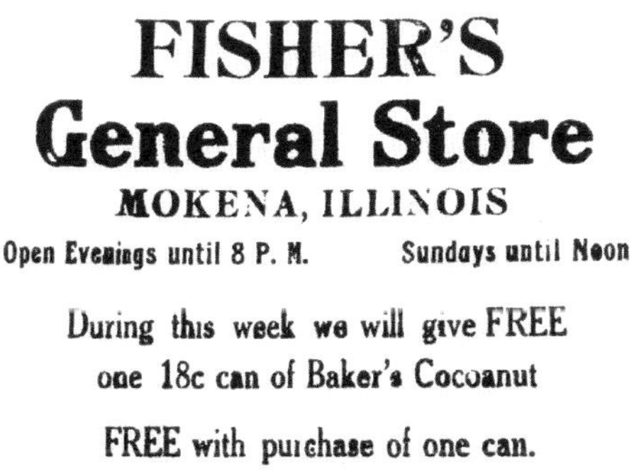

An early advertisement for Walter Fisher's business in Mokena, as it appeared in the August 4, 1922 issue of the *News-Bulletin*. *Author's collection.*

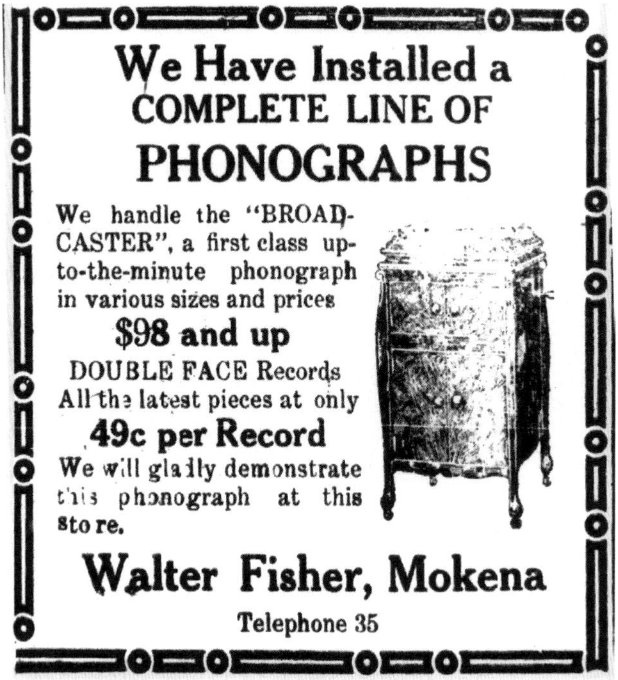

Walter Fisher was a frequent advertiser in the Mokena *News-Bulletin*, this piece from the April 6, 1923 issue being a typical example. *Author's collection.*

In April 1923, Walter relocated his store into a building two doors to the west.[23] Being vacated at the time by Milton and Roy Krapp's Mokena Hardware Company, the structure was a Front Street landmark. In the early 1920s, Mokenians already considered the place old, as it had stood at the site for around sixty years. On the eastern side of the store stood a stately house that was built in the same era, inhabited in 1923 by two elderly, widowed sisters. Walter's new neighbors to the west were two run-down, shabby buildings that had been the source of many local headaches for years. Their stark, foreboding appearance led many Mokena kids to refer to them as the "haunted houses." After the move, editor Semmler wrote in the *News-Bulletin* that Walter was happy in the village and that he would stay permanently, it being "such a good business town."[24] Fisher could be reached at the store under telephone number 35 and kept it open every day until eight o'clock in the evening. He also kept limited Sunday hours, usually until around noon.[25] In this timeframe, an ad of his appeared in a February 1924 issue of the *News-Bulletin* that indicated that Fisher's store kept groceries such as Carmelo sardines packed in tomato sauce from California in stock, while dry goods such as Woolstorm serge and boys' horsehide mittens could also be had. Walter also eventually spruced up some of the store building's upstairs rooms into "cozy flats,"[26] which he rented out to supplement the income for his young family.

That the Fishers were Jews in a small town full of Christians seems to have been of no issue to any of Mokena's residents. Only one recorded incident of open hostility against Walter has survived the years, that being a 1922 fracas involving local butcher Henry Miller. Not long after Fisher's arrival in the village, gossip wafted through town that he had made derogatory comments against Miller's business, namely that he kept his market in dirty shape and that his meat was unsanitary.[27] The butcher accused Fisher of having started the rumor, which he, in turn, denied. Miller's temper flared, and on a July day, he showed up in front of Walter's store, demanding him to come outside and talk with him.[28] Walter refused to leave the safety of his building and instead told Miller that he would gladly speak with him if only he came inside first. Some perceived slight caused Henry Miller to erupt, and "vile names" and a "torrent of cuss words" streamed from his mouth, ending his outburst with threats to run Fisher out of Mokena. A Joliet judge intervened on Walter's behalf and leveled a disorderly conduct charge against Miller, who also was fined $12 and placed under $500 peace bonds for a year. Commenting on the situation in the pages of the *News-Bulletin*, Semmler remarked, perhaps with a smirk, "in the eyes of the law... it is rather expensive to vent your anger and [use] cuss words in public."

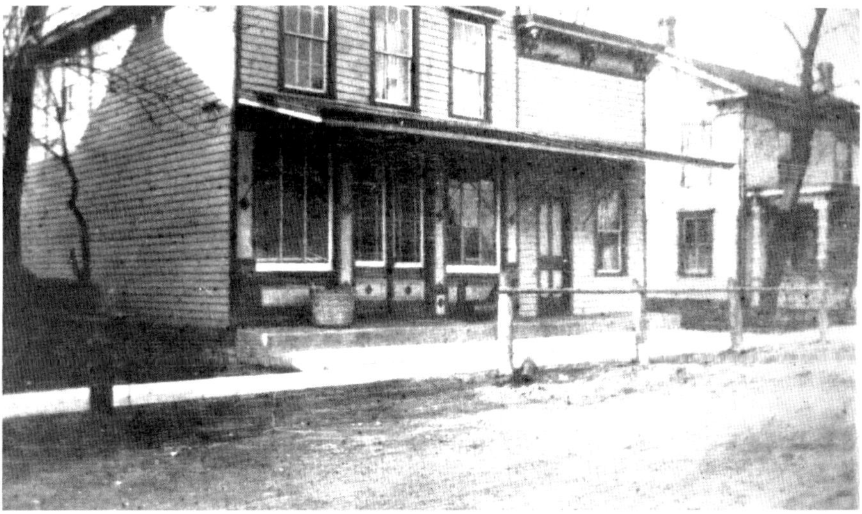

Located on the site of today's 11014 Front Street, Walter Fisher moved his store into this Mokena building in the spring of 1923. *Courtesy Richard Quinn.*

While the entire episode was indeed a nasty one, there are no memories left to indicate that the incident was ethnically motivated.

While Walter Fisher made his living as a merchant, he also served as a Will County sheriff's deputy on the side, work that would come to forge his identity in history. As Mokena had no established police department at the time but, rather, a single appointed police officer, Fisher's deputizing gave the region much-needed support in terms of law enforcement. Walter received his appointment by Will County sheriff John Walker on December 11, 1922,[29] having been a Mokena resident for not quite a year. It wouldn't be long before he made his first arrest. On Christmas Eve, Deputy Sheriff Fisher cuffed a trespassing poacher from Joliet on the Knupp farm outside New Lenox.[30] The man never showed up for his scheduled trial in Mokena that week, with the result that Fisher had to track him down at his workplace in the county seat. The case came and went, and interestingly, when the *News-Bulletin* tried to get the lawman's take on the matter for the paper, he was reluctant to open up, perhaps in a bid to stay out of the limelight.

The majority of what Walter saw while keeping the peace was rather mundane. A typical case was the call he responded to on a fall night in 1924. Around eleven o'clock, he was jarred from his sleep by a "hurry call" from one Agnes Hirsch, who frantically cried that her house was being broken into. On the way to Hirsch's village home in the crisp autumn air, Walter met John Frisch, a Mokena railroad worker who, like himself, had earlier been deputized by the Will County sheriff. Frisch had the additional benefit of being a village-appointed constable. Upon their bleary-eyed arrival at Mrs. Hirsch's, she told them they had just missed the burglar but that he had put his head through her bedroom window.[31]

The maintainer of the Rock Island's railroad signals through the Mokena area, Frisch was old enough to be Walter's father, counting twenty-four years on his younger counterpart.[32] Like his fellow townsman, Frisch was foreign born, having entered the world in the small duchy of Luxembourg. With the end of World War I in 1918, John Frisch demonstrated to Mokena that he was an unquestioned patriot by fashioning a homemade goat costume for his bulldog, upon which he draped a canvas jacket reading "We Got the Kaiser's Goat."[33] Over the course of their tenure as sheriff's deputies, Walter Fisher and John Frisch would come to be frequent partners. While on lookout together in 1923, the two successfully apprehended not one, but two bands of gypsies passing through Mokena who earlier had robbed a Joliet cattle dealer of $160.[34] There was also an episode that same year when the pair happened across a suspicious car parked along the Lincoln Highway at Gougar's Crossing, near New Lenox. Deputy Fisher let the two young gentlemen occupying the car know that they couldn't idle there, and they then continued on. Something didn't sit right with the two deputies, who then investigated a culvert near where the car was standing, only to find fifty pounds of dynamite hidden in it, complete with fuses. They promptly passed word to Sheriff Walker in Joliet, who figured the sticks had been stolen from a contractor.[35] No one ever got to the bottom of who the mysterious men were and why they had secreted the explosives where they did.

The two jobs as both a storekeeper and a deputy sheriff began to make Walter Fisher's plate a little too full for his liking. At the end of December 1923, he turned in his resignation as deputy, telling the *News-Bulletin* that he needed to focus on his "rapidly growing store business." However, in less than a year, he was enticed back to the badge for reasons long since forgotten and was reinstated as a Will County sheriff's deputy by August 1924, when he joined the Illinois Deputy Sheriffs' Association.[36]

After a brazen daytime robbery occurred at the Mokena State Bank in October 1924, Walter swiftly came to the defense of John Frisch after suspicious and incredulous eyes were cast upon him. The period immediately after the heist was one rife with paranoia in town, and a scapegoat was being sought. The Village Board, with a tinge of distrust, questioned Frisch about his association with two fake Prohibition agents who were known in town, men who were thought to have had a hand in the robbery. Specifically, board members were curious as to why Frisch had traded revolvers with one of the men. Walter Fisher appeared in front of the board to deflect any wrongdoing by his neighbor, explaining in his own words that Frisch had "the wool pulled over his eyes" and that "Officer Frisch meant well, but was simply tricked" by the men.[37] After Fisher took the suspects to the county lockup, one of them threatened to exact brutal revenge on him upon his release. The man was banned from the village. Incidentally, the Mokena State Bank was "burglar proofed" a short time after the robbery. Bulletproof steel was installed to back the interior woodwork of the cashier cage, and special 7/8-inch-thick glass was put in to enclose it. At this time, Deputy Fisher was called upon to test the density of this glass, which he did by firing his .38-caliber revolver into it three times. It passed the test.[38]

A noteworthy episode that occurred almost exactly a year prior to the 1924 bank robbery could easily have led to the young merchant-turned-lawman's undoing. It was already after midnight that autumn evening when Walter stepped off a Rock Island train and made his way home. Having spent the day in Chicago, he leisurely went down dark Front Street, all the village's business houses long closed and silent by this time of night. As he headed east, he was aware of a man and woman in front of him traveling in the same direction on the other side of the street. As if from nowhere, an auto from behind Walter sped down the street, destroying the night's silence, and screeched to a halt at the couple, who were standing in front of the Liess bakery. The vehicle's headlights blindingly caught them in their arc, and an unknown man sprung from the car, shouting, "Hold up your hands!" Moonlight glinted off a shiny object in the man's hand. As the two were forced into the auto and the girl's shrieks pierced the air, Walter recognized the girl as nineteen-year-old[39] Marguerite Wachter, the daughter of a local engraver. The screams, the strangers, the shiny object in the man's hand—all of these led Walter to believe he had just witnessed a mugging. He instinctively drew his automatic and put a bead on the man as he disappeared back into the car but stopped just short of pulling the trigger. Instead, as the mystery car sped off, he dashed into his own auto and scoured Mokena, hoping to turn it up again. Before long, he found it at the Wachter house, where, instead of shock and horror, he found a mood of gaiety. The crew piloting the car, among them Marguerite's sister and brother-in-law, were practical jokers. Their "weapon" turned out to be a glass gun.[40]

The episode came to be something of a hot-button issue in Mokena for a brief period that autumn. Walter made a statement to editor Semmler on the front page of the *News-Bulletin* that he was perfectly game for jokes, but in the future to please be more careful. After all, a shooting had only narrowly been avoided that night. Any further "hold-up jokes" would result in prompt arrest. In no time, Marguerite Wachter refuted almost every point of Fisher's version of events: the auto in question wasn't racing down Front Street, there were no screams, no glass gun. The young woman also got her place in the *News-Bulletin*, in which she said that she "enjoyed the joke very much" and that she couldn't see why "we can't have a joke between ourselves without somebody getting all excited" and "making a big story out of almost nothing." With a final barb at Walter, she pointed out that "even if he is a deputy, I think he ought to find out what he is shooting at before he shoots."[41]

Duty often summoned Walter Fisher, and one incident that occurred in March 1923 demonstrated his fearless and heroic devotion to it. In the era before the organized dispatching system used by law enforcement in Will County, Mokena residents directly telephoned Walter when trouble arose. On March 14, he picked up his phone around lunchtime to a stranger's voice telling him that a truckload of illegal beer was due to rumble through the village later that afternoon. In the midst of Prohibition, this was a hot tip, one that couldn't be taken lightly. The mysterious caller clearly had inside knowledge of the people he was betraying; he could have belonged to a rival bootlegging gang. He gave Walter the truck's license plate number and an exact description of the vehicle and reminded him that a blue touring car would be trailing it. In turn, Walter alerted John Frisch, and the two waited at the quiet intersection of Front Street and Wolf Road for the truck.[42] On the southwest corner stood a rickety, low-slung blacksmith shop tucked in among some foliage, while on the two corners to the north stood wooden houses on tree-lined lots. While waiting for the quarry, Frisch cleverly thought to borrow the handheld stop sign of the nearby crossing tender for the Rock Island Railroad.[43]

Around two o'clock that afternoon, the large truck and blue touring car appeared on the horizon just as described. It couldn't get any easier. Frisch waved the stop sign, and the drivers fell for the ruse. Upon their inspection at the crossroads, Fisher and Frisch discovered not only that the autos had originated in Indiana but that the truck's goods looked very promising indeed. One of the men peered under a canvas covering the cargo and spotted two dozen sacks with glass bottles bulging from each one. Inside the truck, the driver was growing more scared by the second; in a desperate, panicked act, he swiftly drew a .42-caliber revolver and aimed at his nearest target: John Frisch. With a cop's instant reflexes, Walter Fisher spotted the gun and wrestled it from the would-be killer, subduing him in the process.

Both drivers were forced to surrender, and the two Mokena lawmen held them in the village for a few hours until Will County sheriff John Walker personally came to town and brought the two men, with their vehicles in tow, to Joliet. Within a few days, word trickled back from the county seat regarding the truck's freight. The bottles had been counted; there were 864 of them, and each contained authentic beer, testing 3.82 percent alcohol. Walter Cash, the truck wheelman who nearly shot Frisch, and Morris Christensen, the touring car's driver, were both placed under $2,000 bonds.

If Walter Fisher's valiant deed that day was recognized by Sheriff Walker, it has been forever lost to time. His most heroic deed as a keeper of the peace, a force of good and a neighbor loomed dreadfully on the horizon.

CHAPTER 3

ALL-AMERICAN BOY

He had buddies everywhere he went, was an inquisitive tinkerer and was a natural at sports. Daniel Ferdinand Hesly's name will forever be linked on the pages of history with that of Walter Fisher. He was born on January 10, 1901, in Chicago, the son of Daniel Hesly Sr. and Bertha Schultz. A native of Alsace-Lorraine in today's France, the elder Hesly arrived as a child in the United States in the aftermath of the Civil War and by 1899 was working in Chicago as a secretary at an electrical firm. In a sign of upward mobility, in his later life, Daniel Hesly Sr. would come to manage a factory.

Dan Hesly Jr. had led a typical Catholic upbringing on Chicago's north side with his doting parents, spending his formative years in a modern home on Carmen Avenue in the Lakeview neighborhood. Dan was the youngest of four children, and that by a long shot; his elder brother Edward was sixteen years his senior, while his sister Rosa was fourteen years older than him. Like Walter Fisher, he grew up surrounded by his ethnic brethren, Lakeview being a center of Chicago's Germanic population. However, unlike Fisher, Dan's childhood was solidly middle class; there is no evidence that he ever knew for want while a lad.

Dan would grow to become a well-known student at Senn High School, where he easily demonstrated a high level of intelligence that must have amazed, if not outright perplexed, his teachers. Words such as "excelled" and "genius" were later used to describe his time at Senn; a friend would later explain that "he was bright in everything he did," while another classmate would say that he was a "wizard at radio." Dan found his niche with amateur radio and was said to be one of the most successful amateur radio operators in the Midwest. A family member would even claim that Dan had designed his own wireless set from scratch.[44]

While gifted with a technical mind, Dan was also a master athlete. He had an aptitude for any sport he set himself to, even winning medals in track and swimming, although it was on the gridiron that he felt most at home.[45] At the strapping age of seventeen, young Dan Hesly was known as a star on the Senn campus, being the lightweight halfback of the school's champion football team.

Although his attendance at school was hit or miss, Dan left Senn High around 1918, with three years completed to his credit.[46] It would later be said that the young man served a stint stateside with the army at this time, feeling the patriotic air common during the era of America's involvement in World War I.[47] While this claim has been difficult to prove with any accuracy, at this time in his life, Dan Hesly was balancing on a narrow line. Those who liked him would easily say he was a very prankish lad and laughingly acknowledge that he could be known to leave a path of mischief in his wake. Others would describe his adolescence as a "trail of boyish theft."

It all began when Dan was fourteen. He made the fantasy of many a boy into reality when he ran away from school, with a group of his friends in tow. Naturally, they would need supplies for their adventure, so Dan swiped some cold cream and toothpaste from a neighborhood store. Before long, he was found out and wept for his mother when faced with his guilt. He returned the stolen goods to the storekeeper, and all was forgotten. This first misadventure would come to be dismissively chuckled at by Bertha Hesly, but others would gradually become more serious. A typical instance was the time Dan and his pals went swimming. Young Hesly wasn't packing a swimsuit, so he disappeared for a bit and, upon his return, had brand-new red trunks hanging off his slender frame. The image was too much for his friends, who laughed him out. Unable to be had by their ridicule, he ditched the red trunks and soon came back a second time wearing blue ones—this time a perfect fit. Both swimsuits were shoplifted from a nearby drugstore.

A good buddy of Dan's helped land him a job at Montgomery Ward's in the city. On his first day, Dan clocked in at 8:00 a.m., but the work was too boring for his taste. Within an hour, he was seen strolling out the door with an elegant fur coat draped around his shoulders. This incident was traumatic for the clean-cut Heslys. This time, his mother was the one who cried, while his father was furious. An early crime landed Dan in the Chicago Bridewell for thirty days on a larceny charge. He completed the sentence without incident and was sent home in the summer of 1918.

At some point in this period, Dan Hesly secured a job at a Chicago key store. It was the perfect playground for the mischievous genius who was already known for carousing about the city with autos that weren't his. He took to fashioning his own keys at the store, and before long, Dan carried a huge key ring that made him look like a prison warden in the eyes of others. His waywardness with cars was leading him to become a familiar face at the Summerdale police station in the city. As a seventeen-year-old, with the country celebrating the end of World War I, Dan and a pal named Donald Buck took the auto of one Samuel Kately on a jaunt. When Kately later recovered his vehicle, he was livid. A future telling of the event would refer to it as a joyride. In the eyes of the law, this was far from the case, and Dan Hesly was walloped with a second larceny charge. This time, his sentence was three months in the Cook County lockup.

A pattern was emerging: Dan was finding himself in and out of jail. Less than a year later, he stood before a judge again and again was slapped with larceny. This sentence was the most serious yet: he faced upward of ten years behind bars. On October 18, 1919, Prisoner #2334 was sent to the Illinois State Reformatory at Pontiac in Livingston County, about eighty-five miles from his Chicago home. Dan put in nearly three years before he was paroled just before Christmas 1922.[48] He had paid his debt to society, mended his ways and stayed out of trouble sufficiently enough to be released from parole in September 1923.

Free again, Dan Hesly went back to radio, his old passion. He aimed to put his hobby to work and was angling to become a radio engineer when he met twenty-year-old Helen Berinski around New Year's Day 1925. Their courtship was passionate and whirlwind, and the couple said their vows to each other on July 25 of the same year.[49] The ceremony was officiated by a justice of the peace in Crown Point, Indiana, a place just over the state line that was known somewhat whimsically as a marriage mill due to its no-waiting policy for couples. Whether Helen knew of Dan's record is unknown, but perhaps in youthful naivety, it didn't matter. The two lovers were now official, and that's all that mattered. They soon settled into a four-room apartment on South Mozart Street in the Brighton Park neighborhood of Chicago.

A baby was also soon on its way to round out the Hesly family, the newest addition being due for summer 1926. With the joy brought into the household, uncertainty and gloom were also looming for Dan. The foray

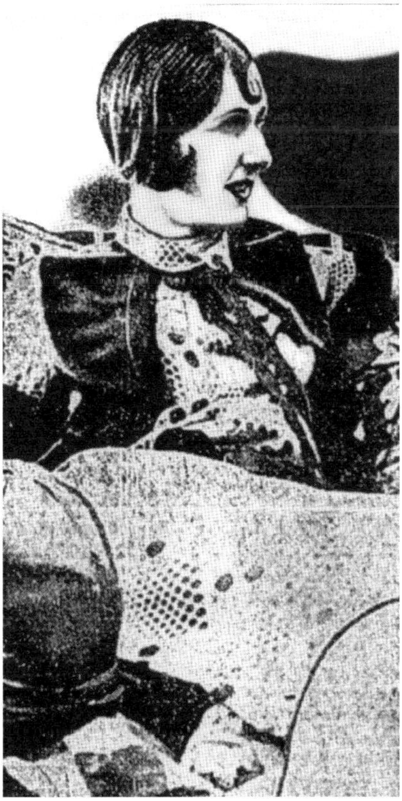

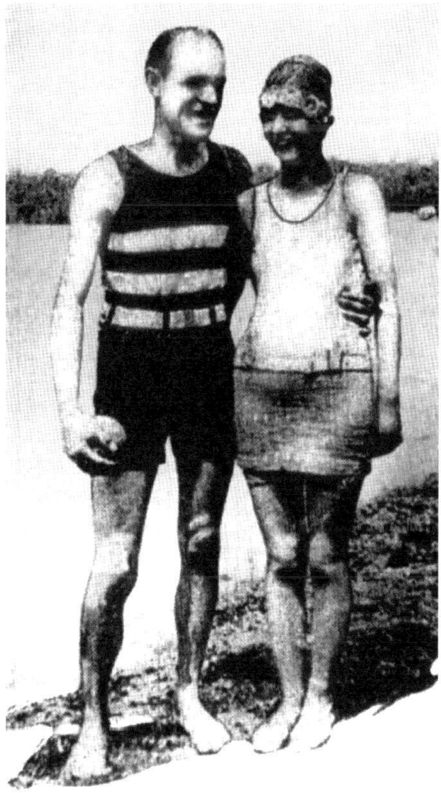

Left: Helen Berinski met Dan Hesly in early 1925 and married him in the summer of that year in Crown Point, Indiana. *Author's collection.*

Right: This candid photo of Dan and Helen Hesly appeared in an April 1926 issue of the *Chicago Daily News*, showing a carefree time before their lives were turned upside down. *Author's collection.*

into radio engineering was proving much less successful than he hoped for himself and his young, expecting wife. In the early months of 1926, he was unemployed. Prospects for him were nonexistent. A bold, drastic step would have to be made. Dan Hesly was the kind of man who liked bold, drastic steps.

CHAPTER 4

BY ANY OTHER NAME

Much like the ebb and flow of time, history has a tendency not to be kind. As years progress, certain facts and the details that belong with them become remembered or, even better, written down and preserved for posterity. Others are rearranged, muddled and contradicted enough to be barely recalled. Ultimately, fate chooses many to be swept into eternal oblivion, like so many grains of sand against a gale. For Santo Ilacqua, most of the fine points of his life have long since been washed away by the tide of ages. To state that little is known of his life compared to those to Walter Fisher and Dan Hesly would be a huge understatement.

His existence remains shrouded in such deep mystery that it is unclear what his actual surname was. Upon this man's brutal end, an Illinois death certificate would be made out in the name Santo Ilacqua, although the document contains a tightly handwritten note, tersely noting, "buried as Calabresi." Whether Ilacqua was an adopted name he acquired at a young age or an alias used for more dubious purposes has been totally forgotten. When the media of his day reported his demise and the grim events associated with it, the name Santo Calabresi was hastily referred to as Santo Calabrese. Therefore, to preserve some sense of regularity in the twists of this man's life, he will be so named in this work.

Those who knew Santo Calabrese would state that he was born around 1889,[50] although even then they couldn't be sure. He was Italian by birth, said to have hailed specifically from a rural locality known as St. Anna de Seminara, located at the southern tip of the country's boot.[51] The surrounding region of Reggio Calabria is a wine-producing one, dotted with mountains and pine forests. It is happily known to the rest of the country as the home of the flavorful, lime-green bergamot orange. Many of the area's residents were tied to agricultural work, and it is likely that Santo Calabrese's early years were also spent in such a pursuit. The long history of the Seminara, as it is known locally, would suffer a permanent black mark when the village was completely laid to waste during a 1908 earthquake.

Years after the disaster, Santo Calabrese found himself on the shores of America. It was 1921, and like waves of other Italian immigrants, Santo would come to call Chicago his home. Upon his arrival in the new country, Chicago boasted of such a large population of Italians that it was known as the third largest city of its kind in the United States, falling only behind New York and Philadelphia in numbers. As was the case with Calabrese, the majority of Chicago's new Italian residents were from the rural, southern portion of the country. Before long, he landed a job working as part of a construction crew[52] in the bustling metropolis, likely a victim of the brutal *padrone* system. Many of the new Italian migrants in Chicago fell victim to this vicious cycle where unscrupulous labor brokers, or *padroni*, enrolled their countrymen in work gangs. Lacking any rights, the workers under the *padroni* lived lives more akin to slaves than those of American craftsmen.

Later documentation would indicate that Calabrese had a wife named Concetta, although some would contradict this and say that the woman was his mother.[53] In any case, Santo Calabrese found residence on Chicago's near west side, first in a place at 1452 Flournoy.[54] By the spring of 1926, he was living at 2263 Wentworth,[55] a little over a mile and a half south of the Loop. It was while Santo lived at this address that a mysterious yet grisly fate found him. Like the enigma that is Santo Calabrese's life, the details of his demise remain muddled by time, although from day one his destiny would be connected to Walter Fisher and Dan Hesly.

CHAPTER 5

APRIL 14

April 1926 did not start well for Mokena. On the first of the month, the Bowman Dairy bottling plant was shut down for a lack of milk, specifically the kind that had been tested free of tuberculosis. Jobs were leaving town, and editor Bill Semmler of the *News-Bulletin* lamented the local mainstay's closing as a "blow" to community.[56] To make matters worse, Mokena and the surrounding area were still reeling in the aftermath of a freak snowstorm that had hit at the end of March.[57] Many of the unpaved, rural roads were completely impassable; the autos of area residents marooned in giant snowdrifts were a common sight leading up to Wednesday, April 14.

Across the state border, the air at Indiana Harbor in Lake County was thick with industry. It was a place of steel mills, one where hard work and commerce abounded. Frank Watson had been a resident of Indiana Harbor for the past three years,[58] and a few months prior, the twenty-two-year-old had taken a job with the Yellow Cab Company. The company was party to a lucrative contract with the Pennsylvania Railroad, in which the firm would ship federal mail from its depot to the Indiana Harbor Post Office.[59] So it was that on the morning of April 14, young Watson was behind the wheel of a truck laden with sacks of mail.

He had picked up two large, stuffed sacks at the Pennsylvania depot as usual. One contained simple registered letters, and the other was full of neatly sorted bundles of cash fresh from Chicago: the payroll of the Inland Steel Company. En route to the post office with his cargo, Watson rounded the corner of Michigan Avenue and Grand Boulevard, aiming to take a shortcut through an alley at the rear of the building to complete the morning's drop-off.

Oddly, Frank Watson noticed a black Chrysler touring car blocking the entrance to the alley.[60] As he brought his truck to a slow stop, the Chrysler's door opened, and out stepped Dan Hesly, wearing a well-pressed dark brown suit with a purple pencil stripe, a dark brown overcoat and a brown hat.[61] Conscious not to appear out of the ordinary in any way, Dan strode over to the idling truck. Before Watson fully comprehended what was about to happen, he felt Dan jam the muzzle of a revolver through his window into his ribs, snarling that he would "shoot to kill" if there was any funny business.[62] He hustled Watson out of the truck and forced him to throw the two mailbags out of it and into his touring car. With force and purpose, Hesly then shoved the young driver into the Chrysler's driver's seat while he took up a defensive position on the seat behind him.

As Frank Watson was forced to drive the strange auto out of the alley, he feared for his life, waiting for the loud report of a pistol to ring out at any second. Under Dan's orders, he steered the touring car south on Grand Boulevard, the revolver trained on him from the back seat. Upon reaching Black Oak Road outside Gary, Hesly drew a straight razor and furiously slashed open at least one of the mail sacks. Like a nesting doll, inside were several smaller canvas bags, each containing dense bundles of cash.[63] He threw the cut-open mail pouch out of the moving auto's window.

Robber and captive continued west toward the Illinois state line, crossing it at Lansing. Nerves aside, Dan Hesly's escape was going remarkably well; as of this point, he hadn't encountered any trouble from the police or a hint of suspicion from anyone. During the swift journey west, Watson stayed cool and kept his wits about him behind the wheel. At least once, he tried to slyly maneuver back eastward in the direction of Hammond. His captor quickly wisened up to the trick though, and a day later, Watson would quip with an air of dismissiveness, "The bandit seemed to know where he wanted to go and made me cut it out."[64]

Watson piloted the cash-laden Chrysler toward Chicago Heights and then westward in the direction of Joliet. All things considered, Dan Hesly began to feel comfortable with his captive. Feeling generous, he offered Watson $200 to "keep with him" and forget about the whole thing once it was done. With his revolver in one hand, his free hand was buried deep in one of the canvas pouches, at one point upping his offer and fishing up a wad of $500. Frank Watson carried on, later explaining Hesly's generosity by quipping, "He said that he found lots of jack in the pouches."[65]

Dan Hesly and Frank Watson had come a long way, putting about thirty-four miles behind them before they came to the outskirts of Joliet, Illinois. Behind the wheel, young Watson was noticing trouble with Hesly's auto. It was acting up in a serious way, and the clutch was slipping. Added to the mix, Watson was also having an increasingly difficult time guiding the vehicle over small inclines. Right after passing through a railroad viaduct in the city proper, the car seized up for good on Cass Street. It was totally broken down. It was nearly 10:00 a.m., and for the first time that day, Dan Hesly's luck was up; the smoothness of the whole operation was gone. However, his fortunes appeared to change in a heartbeat. Like a beacon of light on the horizon, Dan spotted the Ridgewood Service Station, an automotive garage belonging to Charles Larsen, located only a few yards away at 2103 Cass Street.[66] Here he could have his Chrysler quickly serviced, and with luck, his flight could be completed.

Running on adrenaline in light of the auto mishap, Hesly jumped out of the touring car and, along with his captive, Frank Watson, oomphed it into the shop. How exactly the two presented themselves to Larsen's mechanics remains unclear; the fact remains that the workers bought Hesly's ruse, and two of them got to work on the vehicle. Hesly initially managed to keep his cool but fidgeted more and more with each passing minute. Nervous visions flitted through his mind of questions about the mailbags, possible arrival of the police and worse. In his mounting panic, he paid less attention to Watson. The captive driver saw a window of opportunity; freedom from the day's ordeal was within his grasp. When Hesly wasn't looking, Frank cautiously slipped out of the garage. It was around ten o'clock in the morning.[67] When he was sure the former high school athlete didn't notice, he took off into a full sprint, hid behind a neighboring building and urgently started hunting for a phone.

Before long, Dan Hesly looked around and noticed that Watson had disappeared. In a burst of alarm and horror, he reached into the car, grabbed two inner sacks from one of the mail pouches and darted off into a nearby expanse of woods. In his hands, he held $37,000 in cash. Dan's Chrysler was left abandoned at Larsen's with a pair of confused mechanics. Meanwhile, Watson finally managed to find a phone. The first call went to the Joliet police at 10:10 a.m.

Not long after the escape from Larsen's garage, a new act was beginning to play out in Will County.

CHAPTER 6

A SERVANT OF HIPPOCRATES

A contemporary called him "one of the foremost of the younger physicians and surgeons in Will County,"[68] and the morning of the mail heist, Dr. Ernest G. McMahan was on his way toward Mokena—homeward bound. After a childhood spent in Tennessee, McMahan had come to study medicine at Loyola University in Chicago as a young man. In 1923 at the tender age of thirty-one, he moved to Mokena, where he set up his practice, coming to be known affectionately by the townspeople as Doc.

On that Wednesday morning, April 14, he had been called to the sickbed of a patient at Silver Cross Hospital in Joliet.[69] By about 10:30 a.m., he was finished and on his way back home. Dr. McMahan cruised eastward on the Lincoln Highway in his Ford coupe, passing fields and quaint farmhouses. As he got ready to turn left onto the Mokena Road, just under two miles outside town, a well-dressed man stepped out from behind a patch of undergrowth and into the path of his car. He had three sacks in one of his hands; two were paper, and the other one, made of white cloth, was tightly stuffed with square-shaped bundles.[70] The stranger waved him down.

When McMahan stopped his Ford in the country intersection to see what the man wanted, the stranger stepped up to the coupe's door and jerked it open. A day later, the doctor would recall the ensuing exchange. "I want your car," the man barked. McMahan responded first by looking at him in confusion, processing what was undoubtedly an odd request. "What are you talking about?" sputtered the physician. In a flash, the man drew an

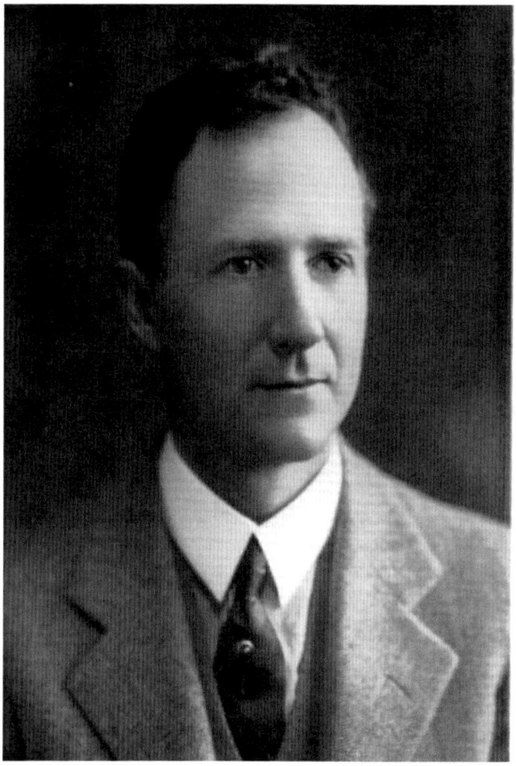

Left: Dr. Ernest G. McMahan was a respected figure in Mokena, whose residents fondly called him "Doc." *Author's collection.*

Below: Near this spot at the modern intersection of Route 30 and Wolf Road in Mokena was the approximate site of Dr. McMahan's carjacking on April 14, 1926. *Author's collection.*

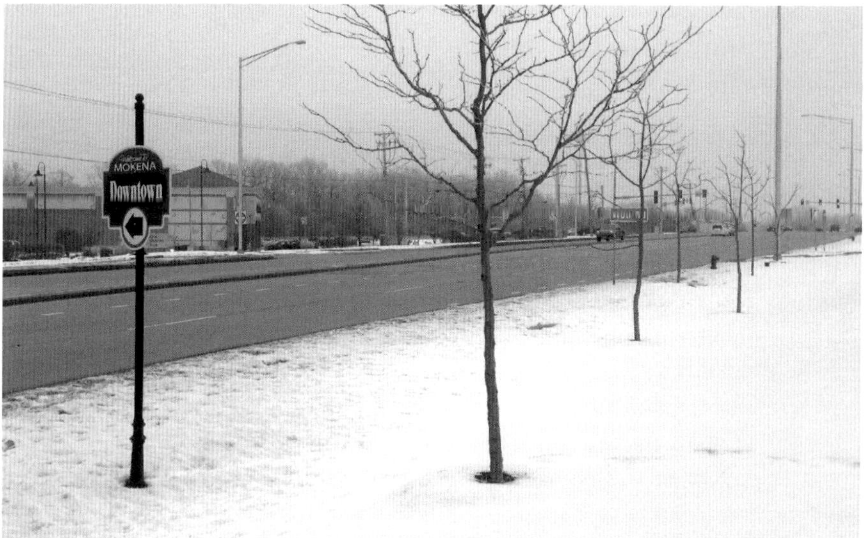

automatic handgun and shoved it into McMahan's side, the barrel's blue steel glinting in the daylight. "Brother, I'm awfully sorry to do anything like that, but circumstances have forced me to do it." The hijacker assured the doctor that he wouldn't hurt him as long as he cooperated. "I'm going to take your car, I need it in my business."[71]

Out of sheer instinct driven by the pistol in his ribs, McMahan jumped out of his Ford while the assailant climbed in. In a moment of clarity, he asked the bandit if he could keep two bags of medical instruments that sat on the passenger's seat, mentioning to the man that they'd really be of no use to him. The bandit tossed out the bags, quickly turned the auto back onto the Lincoln Highway and sped off to the east, disappearing out of sight.

Standing shocked without his car in the rural crossroads, Dr. McMahan dashed across the road to the farmhouse of Clarence Cleveland. McMahan found the farmer and hurriedly explained what had just happened. The doctor promptly made use of the telephone in Cleveland's farmhouse and made two calls to Mokena: one to the auto garage of Cooper and Hostert and the second to Walter Fisher's store. Well aware of Fisher's status in town, McMahan figured he would "get out the deputy to see what he can do."[72]

CHAPTER 7

FISHER'S CHASE

On this Wednesday morning, the Ford agency of Elmer Cooper and Barney Hostert in Mokena hummed with activity as usual. The garage was founded by the two brothers-in-law in 1916, during a heady time when automobiles were rolling off assembly lines and into the mainstream. Fords were repaired and sold from the long, rambling building on Front Street, which, less than a decade prior, was used as a hall for the small village's social arena. Among the day's comings and goings, a phone sprang to life, and thirty-four-year-old Barney Hostert picked up. With the exception of a stint in the army during World War I, Barney had spent his entire life in rural eastern Will County and would have readily known Dr. McMahan when he heard his neighbor's voice on the other end.

"Barney, they held me up and took my car,"[73] the flustered doctor spurted before working in that the bandit was piloting the auto eastward down the Lincoln Highway. With a jolt of urgency from this news, Barney Hostert started a flurry of phone calls from the garage with the same sense of intensity that was taking place at the Cleveland farmhouse two miles to the south. Working with Dr. McMahan's report that the car thief was headed east, Barney placed calls to the Chicago Heights and Homewood police departments. As this informal law enforcement phone tree was being used, Barney's bookkeeper, Florence Hamilton, jumped to inform Walter Fisher in his store three doors to the east. Having likely just heard from the doctor himself, Walter sprang into action with the imperativeness of a defender of the law, grabbing weapons on his way out the door. Later recalling the start

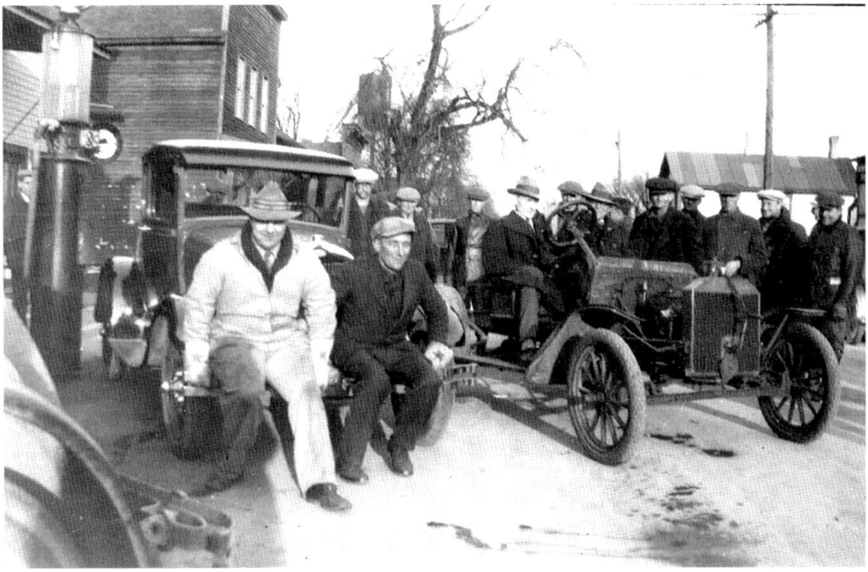

Barney Hostert of Mokena is visible in dark clothing seated on the bumper of the auto in left foreground in this circa 1925 photo. *Courtesy Richard Quinn.*

of the day's action, Barney said, "Fisher came running over with his guns" and commanded, "Let's go."[74]

As the two Mokenians prepared to leave the charged atmosphere of the garage and pick up the chase themselves, Barney took a trusty shotgun and a single shell.[75] If danger confronted him that day, it would be better than nothing.

After McMahan got off the phone with Barney Hostert at the garage in town, Clarence Cleveland, himself a part-time peace officer, set off with McMahan to track down the bandit, the two barreling down the Lincoln Highway in Cleveland's auto. They set off for Chicago Heights, having called the police there ahead of time to let them know what was happening, being unaware that Hostert had already been in contact with them. They happened across some Chicago Heights policemen in Matteson who were sure they were on the right path, as the two then angled though Oak Forest and on to Blue Island.

Meanwhile, in Mokena, another pursuit began. Following the tip on the last known location of Dr. McMahan's car, Barney Hostert swiftly maneuvered his auto out of the tiny village and to the east.[76] Deputy Fisher sat to his neighbor's side, armed and ready at the least to arrest a thief and at the worst for a gun battle. Within minutes, the two arrived at a quiet country intersection, likely today's crossroads of 191st Street and LaGrange Road, known in 1926 as Kean Avenue. Here they waited for their prey, like hunters in a blind. Before long, they spied a vehicle heading past them and to the north. It climbed a hill on the rough gravel road known locally as the Orland Road. Hostert gunned the gas to take up chase behind the car. As their cat-and-mouse chase began in full, the distance between the two vehicles ebbed and flowed. A few days later, Hostert would recall that he and Fisher occasionally got within twenty feet of the suspect.

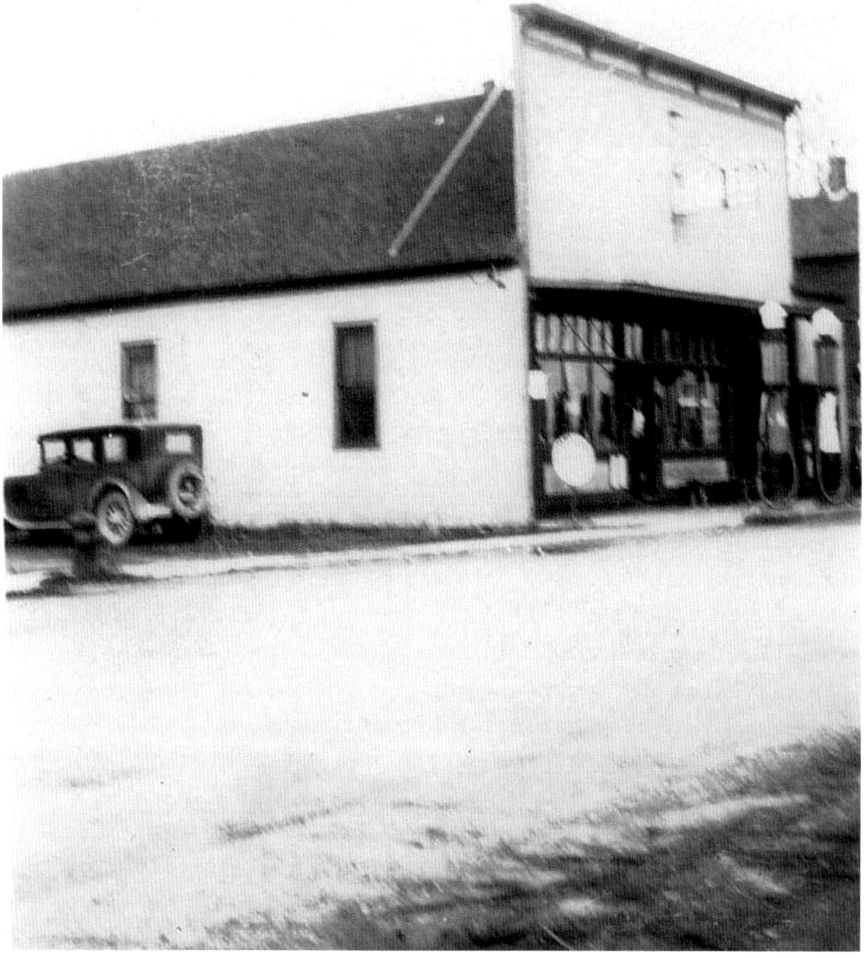

The Cooper & Hostert Ford Agency in Mokena, from where on April 14, 1926, Walter Fisher and Barney Hostert began their pursuit of the auto thief. *Courtesy Richard Quinn.*

The pair scrutinized the auto in front of them as it cut through the rural landscape of fields and farms, occasionally bobbing in and out of sight. While traffic was sparse enough for them to feel safe that this was their man, a positive identification had to be made before any action to seize the car and its hijacker could be taken. The Mokenians had a scrap of paper, upon which one of them had scrawled Dr. McMahan's license plate number, and Walter matched the numbers on the stolen auto with those on the note. Barney knew the car immediately but from a different perspective. He was a man whose life revolved around them, and his eye noticed their nuances in ways that most wouldn't. He spotted a defect in the Ford's bumper and knew it right away.

As the chase carried on over rough gravel and dirt roads with no sign of ending, lawman Fisher and his would-be partner, Hostert, realized that they needed a strategy to end it—a final coup de grace. From their position behind Dr. McMahan's car, they could see through its rear window and could tell that the auto contained only the driver. Their flight from Mokena had been done in the utmost hurry, as not to lose track of their man; as a result, not much planning had been done. In hot pursuit of the bandit, Barney wondered out loud from behind the wheel what exactly they were going to do when they caught up with him. Walter came up with an idea to "stay in back of him until we get on the concrete road,"[77] from whence they would overtake and cut off the car thief.

Deputy Fisher was thinking of the quiet intersection of Kean Avenue and 143rd Street, one known for its distinction of changing from gravel to a solid surface[78] once a driver headed north. As the two cars rolled into the crossroads, they were now almost seven miles north of Mokena and directly to the east of the tiny village of Orland in southern Cook County. What caused the high-speed chase to end here would be disputed by media of the day. One flavorful account stated that Walter leaned out of Barney Hostert's car and shot out the back tires of the doctor's Ford, while Barney said that the auto thief simply came to a stop in front of them.

Regardless of how the halt came, Walter told Barney to pull his vehicle next to the thief's at the intersection. Storekeeper Fisher got ready to draw the pistol he had brought with him. It wasn't the first time he had drawn it in the line of duty for the sheriff's department, and he had every intention of using it to force the unknown outlaw to submit to arrest. As Hostert ground to a stop on the bandit's right, Walter Fisher lunged out of the vehicle, and with one foot on its running board, he covered the man with his pistol and commanded him to "Stick 'em up."[79] They were close enough to have shaken hands.

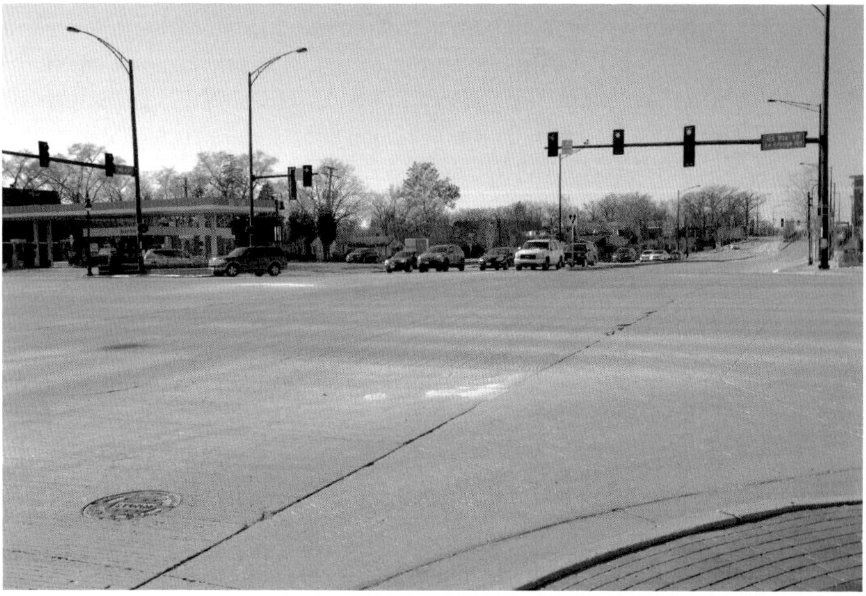

Today's intersection of 143rd Street and Route 45 in Orland Park was the site of the fatal gunfight between Walter Fisher and the auto thief. *Author's collection.*

The adrenaline-surged thief was quicker. In a flash, he drew his own gun and blasted Walter back into Barney Hostert's auto, his body shredded by six steel-jacketed rounds. Two tore through his liver and one ripped open his chest, while others buried themselves in his shoulder, arm, right leg and foot. As Fisher crumbled backward into his neighbor's car, he managed to blindly blow off five rounds of his own, all directed at the bandit in McMahan's Ford. Mere inches away from Fisher, Barney Hostert felt a sting of showering glass as the bandit's shots rang out. He instinctively dove under his steering wheel and, within seconds, managed to crawl out of the driver's door for cover. The shooter ditched Dr. McMahan's vehicle and fled into a nearby field, leaving a crimson trail behind him, one that showed that some of Walter's adrenaline-fueled shots had found their mark. He threw away his empty shells under a willow tree,[80] reloaded and laid low for a few minutes.

Blood-smeared and weak, Walter slid out onto the running board of Barney's car. As he was rolling out, the part-time cop gurgled to his partner, "He got me, get help." These were the sad last words of a hero. Within a few seconds, his massive blood loss would cause him to slip into total unconsciousness. Aware that the gunman was gone, Barney took off on foot to a nearby farmhouse. As history isn't always kind to details, it's been lost to

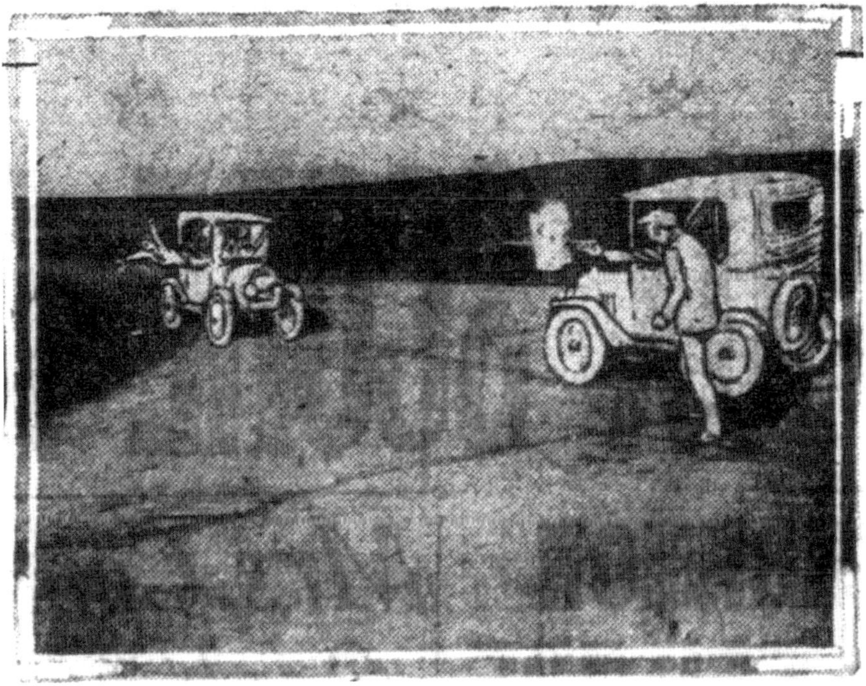

This stylized and factually incorrect rendition of Deputy Fisher's murder appeared in the April 15, 1926 issue of the *Chicago American. Author's collection.*

time exactly what he told the residents of the house; also long since forgotten are their names and the location of their home. What is clear is that they helped Barney Hostert place a phone call into Orland to the office of Dr. Walter Schussler, the neighborhood physician.

To make matters worse for the shaken-up auto man, Dr. Schussler turned out to not be home. Mindful of the fact that Dr. Ernest McMahan of Mokena was carrying on his own hunt with Clarence Cleveland through southern Cook County, Barney then telephoned Dr. W.V. Hedges of Frankfort. With gloom-leaden poise, he explained the situation to the doctor, who set out for Orland to tend to the gravely shot Fisher. As the doctor was on his way, Barney set out to return to the deputy, not knowing if he was dead or alive. After the gunfight, Barney discovered that he, too, had been wounded, albeit much less seriously than his Mokena neighbor. A splinter of lead or shard of his auto's glass had clipped the edge of his nose when the bullets flew.

A Blue Island candy salesman by the name of Raack was in Orland that day on business. While at the Schmaedeke general store at Beacon Avenue

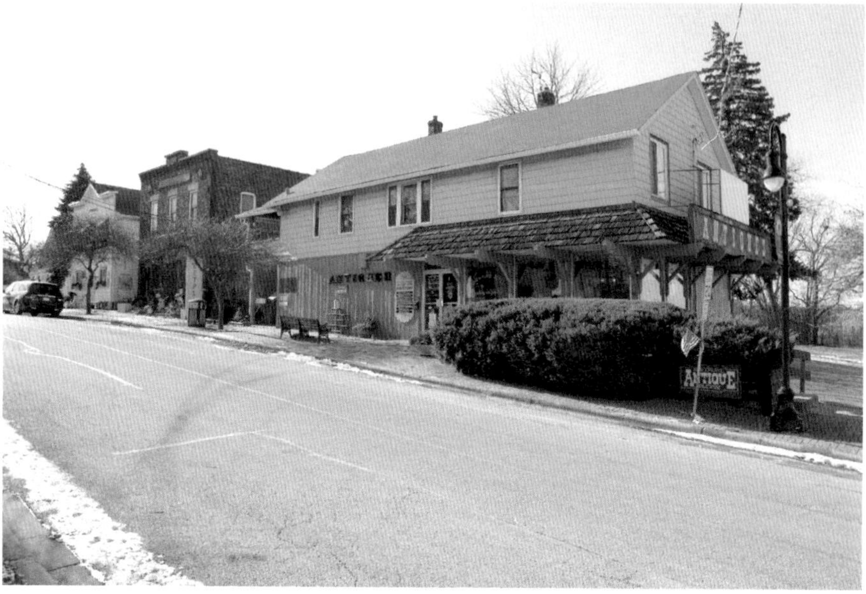

The location of the Schmaedeke store in Orland Park at 143rd Street and Beacon Avenue, where gunshots were heard. *Author's collection.*

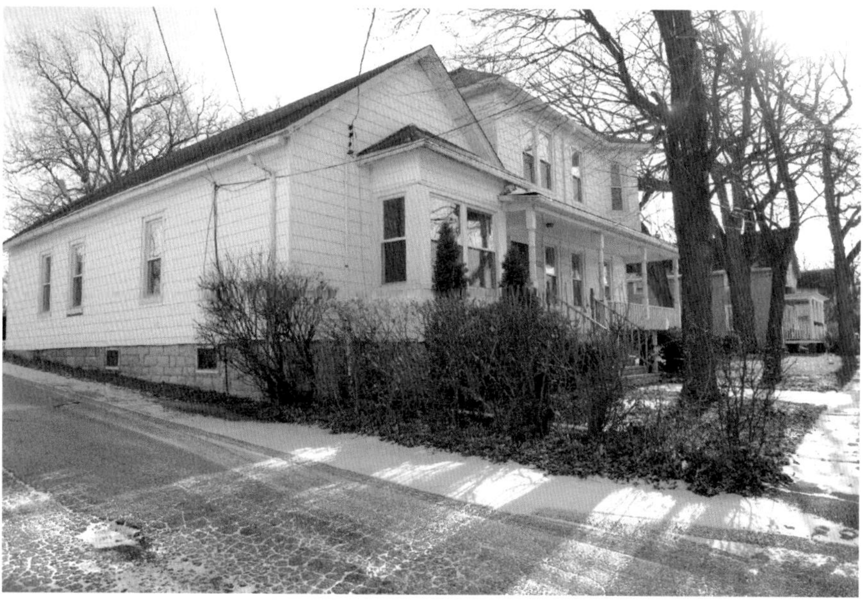

The former residence and office of Dr. Walter Schussler on Orland Park's Beacon Avenue. It was here that Deputy Fisher died after the fatal shooting. *Author's collection.*

and 143rd Street, roughly a quarter of mile away, he heard the fusillade and bravely came to investigate the bloody intersection in his Dodge coupe.[81] Raack and Barney Hostert got to the crossroads at about the same time, and the Mokenian was shocked to see that the bandit had returned to the scene and restolen McMahan's car, speeding off while Walter lay there. The garage owner and salesman found Walter on the hard, rough road, out cold in a crimson pool. While unconscious, he still showed distant signs of life.

The two gingerly loaded the shot lawman into Raack's Dodge and made for Dr. Schussler's office a short distance away in the village of Orland. In a matter of seconds, they made it to the doctor's Beacon Avenue office, housed in a small attached wing of Schussler's residence. While Frankfort's Dr. Hedges was making his way to Orland at breakneck speed, Barney Hostert and Raack carried Walter into the empty office. He was fading fast, the lifeblood being literally drained from his body as the garage man and candy salesman stood over him helplessly. The fact that the doctor wasn't in was starting not to matter.

Walter Fisher bled out at Schussler's office. It was the end of his watch, the sounding of a reveille. In an ultimate irony, his was a helpless death at a doctor's office with no physician to attend to him. Back in Mokena, Ethel Fisher received a phone call. She ended it with a hair-raising scream, one so bloodcurdling that it resonated in the mind of her daughter for the next seven decades.[82]

CHAPTER 8

DOOM'S CHARIOT

On April 14, 1926, law enforcement authorities across Chicagoland were completely keyed in to the day's events, with the massive robbery across the Indiana border and the murder of Deputy Fisher just outside Orland registering immediately on their collective radar. In regard to the heist at Indiana Harbor, the *Lake County Times* reported, "Within an hour after the robbery, every city and town in the middle west had been appraised of the banditry." Authorities waited at strategic roads on the outskirts of Chicago for Walter Fisher's killer, while by the night of the fourteenth, police and postal inspectors were said to be "closing in around the woods north of Joliet" for then-unknown Dan Hesly and his loot from the earlier mail robbery.[83] At this early stage, the industry of northwest Indiana went into a state of damage control, believing that Inland Steel wasn't the only victim of the robbery and that many businesses had lost money. As the dust settled, this fear was quickly debunked.

When it came to covering the shooting of Walter Fisher, the evening papers were full of wild inaccuracies that reflect the haste with which facts were gathered. One report placed the gunfight near Chicago Heights, at a location fourteen miles from its actual site, while elaborating that a Henry Fisher died on Ridge Road after taking fire from a black car.[84] There was even initial confusion as to the cause of Deputy Fisher's demise, with one Chicago paper stating that a head wound did him in.

With the facts still being straightened out, the next gruesome chapter in the saga of April 14 played out near Melrose Park, when a Bellwood policeman made an unusual discovery. Officer James McBride was headed south on Wolf Road a touch outside Melrose Park when he spotted it. He couldn't be sure if it was around 1:00 p.m. or closer to 1:25 p.m., but when McBride stepped up to the abandoned Ford coupe, he was almost exactly twenty-one miles north of the spot on Kean Avenue where Walter Fisher was gunned down—a crime that he was still unaware of.

Earlier, while at the village hall of Bellwood in Proviso Township, Officer McBride took a call from a local hardware store, where a farmer had mentioned something about a suspicious car in a field that was riddled with what looked like bullet holes.[85] The derelict auto had been spotted perched precariously in a ditch on the west side of Wolf Road, about eight hundred feet north of Lake Street, within sight of a schoolhouse where class was in session. McBride realized this spot was just outside his Bellwood jurisdiction, and while it was indeed a little closer to Melrose Park, the responsibility for the coupe was that of the Cook County police.

Perhaps to secure what looked like a crime scene, but possibly also out of boredom, the young policeman[86] decided to drive to the mystery car to investigate. Finding it within minutes, James McBride was greeted by a gory scene. Not only was one of the Ford's windows completely shattered, but the windshield was flecked with blood, as were the auto's left running board, back fender and interior seats. He found the driver's door punctured by two gunshots, a shot-out brake light and a noticeable quantity of mud inside the vehicle. The crimson stains and bullet holes gave mute testimony to foul play having happened in the car. It was clear—whoever had last driven this car had been shot.

Officer McBride "looked it over" and, aside from determining that the vehicle was out of gas and had an engine that was still warm, wasn't able to find any other evidence after having searched through the brush around it. He visited a nearby farmhouse to see if anyone at home had seen anything suspicious in regard to the Ford, and while they hadn't, the farmer said that an hour earlier, the auto hadn't been there. In the meantime, McBride's Melrose Park colleagues towed the abandoned car to their jurisdiction and sent out bulletins to Chicago to check every doctor's office and hospital for any seriously wounded people. While following up on the coupe's license plate number with a Chicago authority, Officer McBride got news of Walter Fisher's slaying earlier that morning, remembering him a few days later as "the Sheriff of Will County."

That night, every inch of the bloody auto was examined by fingerprint experts.[87] Confusion in the case only deepened when it was discovered that

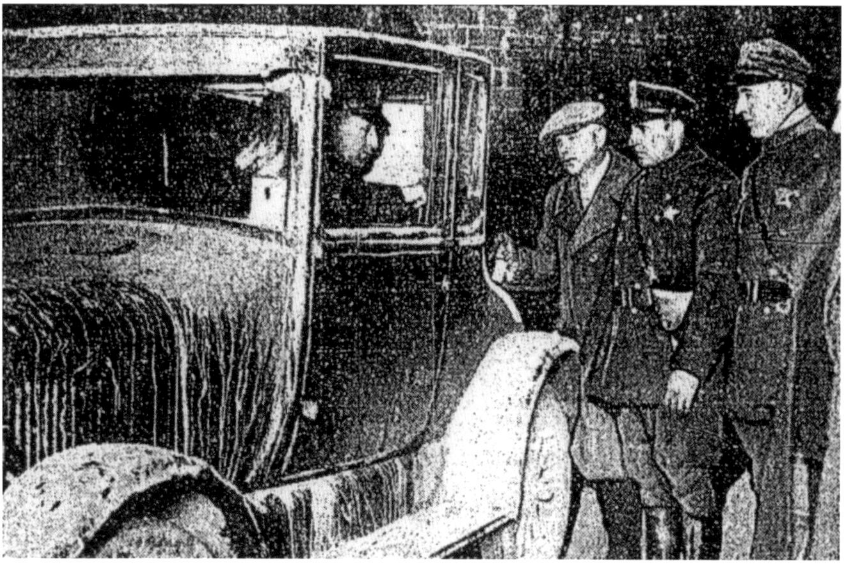

In an image that appeared in the *Chicago Tribune*, law enforcement officials are seen with Dr. McMahan's recovered Ford coupe on the evening of April 14, 1926. *Author's collection.*

the plates didn't match the car. A preliminary investigation that day tracked them back to their owner, W.M. Brown of East End Avenue in Chicago,[88] but Brown explained that the Ford coupe wasn't his; the plates must have been switched at some point after his vehicle had been stolen previously. Reports were cross referenced for other stolen autos, and at the end of the night, Dr. McMahan got a telegram in Mokena stating that the chief of police in Melrose Park had found his Ford coupe.[89]

CHAPTER 9

"A GRUESOME DISCOVERY"

After Al Hruby got the panicked reports from three customers who had just left his roadhouse that there was a bloody, crumpled heap in Twenty-Second Street a few blocks from his place, he decided to investigate with two buddies, Fred Karpel and Charley Rimek. As Hruby got out of Karpel's open-top car and approached the neatly dressed corpse of Santo Calabrese that night, he saw a shattered figure—one that had been completely riddled by bullets and whose head had been ruthlessly crushed, likely by the unseen car tire that left a grisly smear in the road with Calabrese's blood. In the night's darkness, the restaurant owner couldn't tell whether Calabrese, lying on his side, was alive or dead. Lacking a better idea, Hruby heaved the lifeless form off the asphalt into Fred Karpel's auto, bunching up Calabrese's overcoat under his smashed-in head for good measure.

At around 11:30 that night, and from that spot between Third and Fourth Avenues, Hruby, his friends and their grim cargo rushed the short drive to Broadview's Speedway Hospital at Ninth Street and Roosevelt Road. Along the way, they were intercepted by Broadview police officer Joe Huszar in his Ford coupe; he had already received a report of the body. The group made it to Seventeenth and Twenty-Second Streets, where they halted and spoke to the lawman, to whom Hruby glibly uttered, "Joe, the fellow looks bad."[90] Still unaware of how Calabrese had received his wounds, Huszar escorted them to the hospital, where another officer examined the man upon arrival and declared him to be dead.

Before a doctor could wheel away Calabrese's body, Huszar attempted to gain some sort of gleaming as to his identity. Among $1.10 in cash, a pocketknife, a razor and a pawn receipt that turned out not to be Calabrese's, Huszar also came up with the key to cracking his identity: an October 1924 telegram receipt to Europe bearing Calabrese's full name.[91] His old address, 1452 Flournoy Street on Chicago's south side, was also found among his pocket litter. Standard fingerprinting was done of the corpse's hands, which sealed the identity.

After the deposit of his remains to the morgue, the grim duty of the postmortem examination began. Aside from the skull damage done by the car that ditched him on Twenty-Second Street, Calabrese's body was found to have been pierced by at least three bullets. The fatal round was determined to have been fired into his head by an unknown killer, while two other superficial bullet holes were found to be in his back and hand.[92] Oddly, the lesser wounds were off a different caliber handgun than the headshot, and as the details of the entire episode made their way into the Chicago papers, Sergeant William Bokholdt of the Cook County Highway Police nonchalantly mentioned to the *Chicago Daily News* that "the wounds in the back and the hand undoubtedly were inflicted by the deputy sheriff who chased him from Mokena to Orland." Thus, with a painful lack of further detail appearing on the historical record, it came to be that Santo Calabrese was not only named the killer of Walter Fisher, but in the following days, he was also called the perpetrator of the Indiana Harbor mail heist.

CHAPTER 10

MOURNING IN MOKENA

The news of Deputy Walter Fisher's brutal murder appeared in papers as far away as Arizona and New York and gained especially prominent coverage throughout the Chicago region. While the media devoured the story, the village of Mokena was cast under a pall. The pain of his untimely death was localized in the community like an open wound, while just down the road, the *Joliet Herald News* stated that "the town of Mokena is in mourning." After having already covered so much of Walter's career of the previous few years, home paper editor William Semmler used his *News-Bulletin* as a pulpit to eulogize his fellow townsman, and his words were robust:

> *Walter Fisher died a game fighter in his duty as a deputy sheriff of Will County. He laid his life down to protect the property and lives of the neighbors and friends of his community. He was a real man and hero in every sense of the word and this community should always revere his memory. He was such a staunch supporter of law enforcement that he did not hesitate to die to uphold the law.*

Writing from a position of rage at having violently lost his neighbor, Semmler also referenced the lawless feeling of the era:

> *We deplore his tragic death but hope that he did not offer his life in vain, but rather that it will the more spur on the people of Will County to demand*

> *that the laws be strictly enforced in this county, if this is not done the time will be sure to come when the public will execute every outlaw summarily without resorting to any legal process for many of these murderous outlaws are pardoned and turned loose on society again.*

The front-page piece ended poignantly, coming from a place within Semmler's heart: "Walter Fisher was a good citizen, business man, kind neighbor, faithful friend and loving husband and father. He was big hearted, ever ready to do a good deed. May his reward be rich in the life he has now entered beyond."

In keeping with Jewish custom, Walter's body was buried within twenty-four hours of his passing. His family and friends, including a crowd of Mokena residents, assembled at two o'clock on April 15 at Chicago's Weinstein Chapel,[93] located near Garfield Park at Roosevelt Road and Independence Boulevard. After a ceremony performed by Rabbi Envin of Joliet, Walter's earthly remains were interred in a simple plot at Waldheim Cemetery, a series of mammoth Jewish graveyards just west of Chicago city limits in Forest Park. Over time, a large marble headstone would come to hold watch over Walter's bones there, one that bears witness to not only profound sadness but also undying love, bearing as much pathos today as the day it was created. Walter Fisher's name is etched in stone within the motif of a heart, bearing a dual-language English and Hebrew inscription. So it came to be that Walter Fisher belongs to the ages.

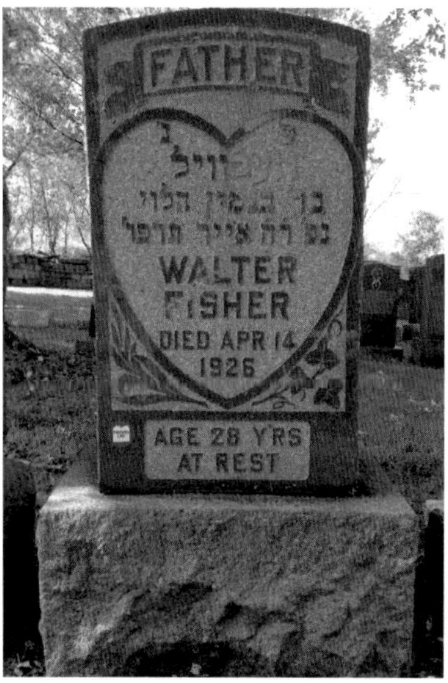

Standing eternal guard over Deputy Fisher's remains is this poignant tombstone at Waldheim Cemetery in Forest Park, Illinois. *Author's collection.*

Exactly one week later, on April 22, another burial occurred. Six miles to the west of Waldheim, Mount Carmel Cemetery in Hillside received the body of Santo Calabrese, the man who had been assigned the blame as Walter Fisher's murderer. As the player of a tragic bit part in an even sadder story, time has not recorded whether anyone paid any attention to Calabrese's entombment, nor does it appear that his final resting place was ever marked in any meaningful way.

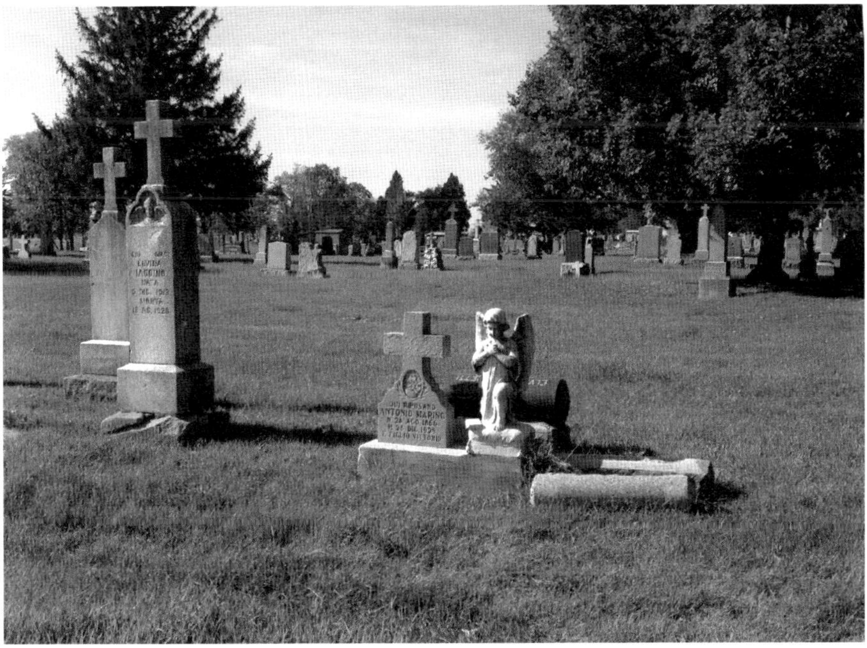

Santo Calabrese was buried in this section of Mount Carmel Cemetery in Hillside, Illinois. As of this writing, his grave is unmarked. *Author's collection.*

As the two men met unnatural deaths, coroner's inquests had to be carried out into the demises of Santo Calabrese and Walter Fisher. The lawman's was held on April 15, 1926, at the Fredricks & Hayes Chapel, an undertaking establishment at 7444 Archer Avenue in Summit. Convened by Deputy Coroner F.H. Guffin and a jury of eight locals, the proceedings seem to have been a hurried and confused manner, with unnamed voices calling out answers and numerous questions being repeated. At one point, star witness Barney Hostert even showed up late due to his having gotten lost. As part of the inquest's business, the jurors viewed Walter's body at the establishment, and various topics were scrutinized, such as his financial assets and the value of his estate in Mokena, to which one participant glibly remarked, "He owes more debt on his property than the property is worth." Queried as to Walter's physical condition while alive were his grief-stricken father and brother, Ben and Max Fisher of Chicago. They were asked the level of education Walter had reached, as the jury also sought basic information on his wife, Ethel, and the ages of his children. Dr. McMahan gave his account of the theft of his car outside Mokena, and Barney Hostert also spoke before the jury and, in long testimony, gave what is probably the most detailed recorded account of the chase with the car thief and Walter's ultimate death.

The same day, an inquest was convened over the remains of Santo Calabrese at the Speedway Hospital in Broadview. Named for the old racetrack on which it was built, the hospital hosted witnesses Albert Hruby and Officer Joseph Huszar for the business with Calabrese's body in the morgue. This inquest was a much more focused affair, detailing the exact condition of the corpse as it was found by Hruby, as well as seemingly mundane affairs such as what kind of hat he had found next to the body in Twenty-Second Street. Perhaps tellingly, Officer Huszar was quizzed about the fact that he had happened across two suspicious cars at the scene where Calabrese would be dumped about a half hour beforehand. Dr. McMahan's bullet-riddled and bloodstained Ford coupe had also been brought to the hospital, where jurors were guided through the trajectories of the projectiles that struck it during the brief, fatal shootout in Orland.

That day, a parade of people was summoned from different areas of Chicagoland in order to formally identify the corpse. April 15 found Constantino Furiano of Wentworth Avenue face to face with the body; as Santo Calabrese's landlord, he recognized him immediately. Two other Chicagoans, Dominic Trumpli and Jess Olivo, backed up his claim.[94] For good measure, authorities kept the three men until early on April 16, fruitlessly grilling them in an attempt to gain insight into Calabrese's activities. The men were of no help and claimed to barely know him, although they were able to roughly guess that he was about thirty-seven and remembered something about him having a brother in New York.

Two more participants in the day's grim parade were Mokenians Barney Hostert and Dr. Ernest McMahan. For Barney, the corpse's face was too bloody to be completely sure, but the coat and hat of the man who shot Walter matched up about right with Calabrese's. McMahan's identification was much more emphatic. In regard to the body before them and the theft of his car the day before, during questioning at the inquest McMahan recalled, "I talked to him. Looked at him carefully. I think I could recognize that face."

After a long day of questioning the varied witnesses, it was agreed to reconvene Santo Calabrese's and Walter Fisher's inquests fifteen days later, this time at the town hall in Summit. What began as a murky situation, especially in regard to Calabrese, only got more chaotic at two o'clock on April 30. The cases of both men were clearly identified as homicides;

however, during the second part of the inquest, a dramatic, unseen U-turn occurred in the testimony of two key witnesses. The men from Mokena, Barney Hostert and Dr. Ernest McMahan, officially withdrew their original statements and stated for the record that the auto thief and gunman they encountered was actually not Santo Calabrese but Dan Hesly.

CHAPTER 11

CUFFED

After Dan Hesly's frenzied escape from the Ridgewood Service Station in Joliet, there remained a large chunk of unaccounted time in his day's timetable. His exact whereabouts during the period between the theft of Dr. McMahan's auto outside Mokena and the shooting of Deputy Walter Fisher near Orland Park have never been clearly explained. Hesly next showed up on the proverbial radar that afternoon in a taxi in Park Ridge, Illinois, a community about fourteen miles northwest of Chicago's Loop, where he appeared to have been on the way to the home of his mother, Bertha Hesly. Still teeming with nerves and paranoia from the payroll heist that morning, Hesly asked the taxi driver if he couldn't drive around the area for a little while, ostensibly to shake any unknown followers who might be in tow.

Upon passing an empty gas station, Hesly asked the driver to let him out. The fare came out to $5.75, and as the cabbie jerked the arm of his meter, he noticed that his passenger had slit open one of the large canvas sacks that he was lugging. He watched as Hesly peeled off a $10.00 bill from within, adding that he should keep the change. While the $4.25 tip was a classy move on Hesly's part, the *Chicago Tribune* would later understatedly call it a "minor slip." Something about such a generous gratuity didn't sit well with the driver. Following his better instinct, he reported the suspicious act to the police,[95] which set in motion a chain of events that led to Dan Hesly's downfall.

Meanwhile, shortly after the heist and for the time being safely ensconced in Park Ridge, Hesly secreted his loot by carefully placing huge sums equaling $24,000 of the total $37,000 in safe-deposit boxes in a local bank, while the rest of the cash was deposited in a box at the National Bank of the Republic in the heart of Chicago's financial district on LaSalle Street. To err on the side of caution, Dan stuffed a few hundred more dollars in a barrel behind his mother's home, as well as having passed her around $300, begging the question of what exactly he told her about its origin. In terms of himself, Dan and his expectant wife, Helen, briefly lay low at her mother's house at 2912 West Fortieth Place in Chicago's Brighton Park neighborhood. This was just a way station, as their ultimate destination became the new Morrison Hotel, a high-rise at Clark and Madison Streets in the city's downtown. The two registered under the fake names of Mr. and Mrs. Charles Coe and checked into room 3026.

Law enforcement officials had been on Dan Hesly's tail since the first second of the robbery at Indiana Harbor, resulting in what the media would call "day and night work by a small army of postal inspectors."[96] After word of a lavish tipper in the Chicago area hauling huge canvas sacks made its way to authorities, they were somehow able to quickly hone in on Hesly. One of their first acts was to speak with Bertha Hesly, who not only innocently told them that her son had come into some money as of late but also let slip his home address on Mozart Street, which was quickly placed under covert surveillance.

Among the investigators whose noses were to the grindstone were Postal Inspectors G.F.H. Birdseye of Cincinnati and Grant B. Miller of Chicago. According to what they later told the press, the two gumshoes came up with a trick to lure Hesly out into the open. The feint involved leaking a red herring to the newspapers, in which the investigators stated that they more or less had their man. In time, Inspectors Birdseye and Miller would proudly state that they had woven the story of Santo Calabrese's gangland murder into a false narrative of his being not only the mail robber but also Deputy Fisher's killer. They would come to confidently, yet without any recorded explanation, tell the media that postal investigators had pieced together Dan Hesly's guilt within twenty-four hours of the heist.

Exactly a week after the caper in Indiana Harbor, on April 21, 1926, a veritable squad of law enforcement, including policemen belonging to Chicago's detective bureau and inspectors under the command of Birdseye and Miller, descended on the Morrison Hotel. There they lay like lions in the brush, waiting for their prey. Their painstaking sleuthing had led them there;

in fact, earlier that day, all but $7,000 of Dan Hesly's loot had been scooped up by them from the bank boxes where it had been stashed.[97] Knowing he'd show up at any second, they ordered the Morrison's exits quietly sealed off, and as husband and wife entered their room that day, Dan Hesly was cuffed.

The day after Dan's arrest, Bertha Hesly hosted a group of her son's friends, his wife and a *Tribune* reporter at her Park Ridge home.[98] The conversation revolved around the young man whose life had previously been one of mischief and occasional illegal misconduct, one that had taken a much darker turn since he pulled off the mail heist he was being shouldered with. As the crowd sat in the "spotlessly neat" living room of the Hesly home, the conservation was light at first and even filled with laughter, as Mrs. Hesly highlighted her son's early achievements with radio as well as his high marks at school and even scoffed off the early features of his criminal career. However, the lighthearted atmosphere bred a gloomy one. The reporter present in the room somberly noted that Bertha Hesly "cried at the thought of how futile all her work for him had been." In the days after Dan Hesly's April 1926 crimes, any commentary from his father remained noticeably absent in the narrative.

The same reporter also had some facetime with Dan's wife, Helen. She was much less vocal, saying only that she took pity on him and wondered aloud what would happen once their baby was born that summer. Lorraine Constance Hesly entered the world on June 8, 1926, in Cook County.[99] It's safe to say that her father wasn't present for her birth.

CHAPTER 12

IN THE FACE OF FATE

On April 21, 1926, the same day he was arrested at the Morrison Hotel, Dan Hesly was swiftly rushed out of Chicago over the Indiana border to Lake County, the scene of his robbery in Indiana Harbor.[100] In a whirlwind, he sat before a federal commissioner in Hammond, was arraigned and had his bail set at $50,000. During interrogation that day, Hesly freely admitted to being the man behind the heist. Nonetheless, the same day, word first reached the press that the Chicagoan was a suspect in Deputy Fisher's slaying in Orland Park.

In explaining the bustle of their prisoner over the Indiana state line, postal inspectors made it clear that it was done in order to be one step ahead of Chicago police, who at this early point were gunning to charge Hesly for Fisher's killing the week before. As would become common in this case, no specific evidence made its way to the media directly tying Hesly to the murder.

By the evening of the twenty-first, none of the colossal bail for Dan Hesly had been posted, and thus, he landed in the jail at Crown Point, the county seat of Lake County, and also the town where he had tied the knot with Helen less than a year before. On his way into the lockup, he was intercepted by a reporter from the *Lake County Times* who was struck by Hesly's cavalier attitude, having noted that he "joked with government detectives, kidded the United States marshal and whistled 'The Prisoner's Song'" as he was being led into his cell.[101] (From the melancholy perspective of an inmate leaving his lover, the song was one of the most popular of the decade.)

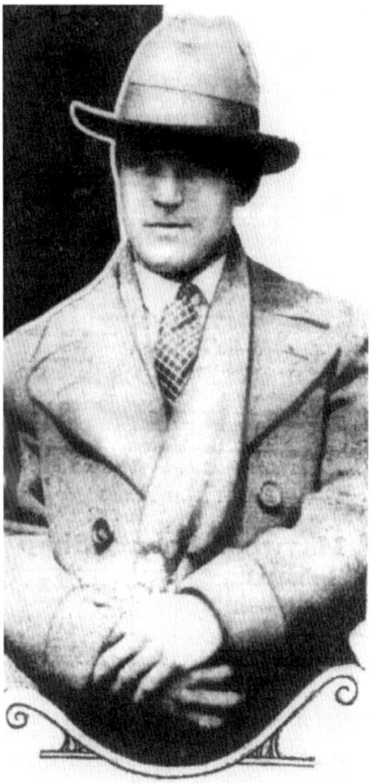

A shackled Dan Hesly is seen here as he appeared in the *Lake County Times* on April 22, 1926. *Author's collection.*

Contrasting Hesly's cocky air, his jailer painted a different picture, telling the *Times* that the accused robber was a "a cynical, unemotional, cold-eyed 'bad man' of the new school." The reporter managed to speak with Hesly himself, having posed him the hackneyed question of whether it paid to be a bandit. Hesly let a sarcastic smile slip and dodged the inquiry by glibly saying, "Don't be a small town guy." Upon being grilled for an answer that made sense, he granted the reporter a peek behind the façade he was putting up for those who saw him that day and gloomily said, "Well, it didn't pay me very big, did it?"

With Dan Hesly behind bars in Crown Point, a major turning point in the chronicle reared its head, one of such extreme significance that everything in the case would drastically change from that point on. The initial identification of Santo Calabrese's corpse by Barney Hostert and Dr. McMahan as the man they saw on April 14 immediately became moot as soon as Dan was in custody. He was presented to them in a lineup in Crown Point on April 23, at which time they positively identified him as the auto thief and murderer of April 14.[102] When the two Mokenians were face to face with Hesly, they pegged him as the man, therefore rescinding their previous statements in regard to Calabrese. Even before the Crown Point lineup, McMahan had readily picked out a photo of Hesly from among fifty others at the Federal Building in Chicago.

At the continuance of Deputy Fisher's inquest on April 30, Hostert was specifically asked what caused him to change his identification. Referring to the body of Calabrese that he had seen previously at the Speedway Hospital in Broadview, Hostert candidly said, "Well, the only thing is, his face was all blood. You couldn't see. But this man what we went to [see at] Crown Point named Hessley [*sic*] had the same clothes on" as the man who shot Fisher. He also went on to say that Calabrese was a little on the heavy side to have been the killer. When pressed on his positivity in regard to Hesly,

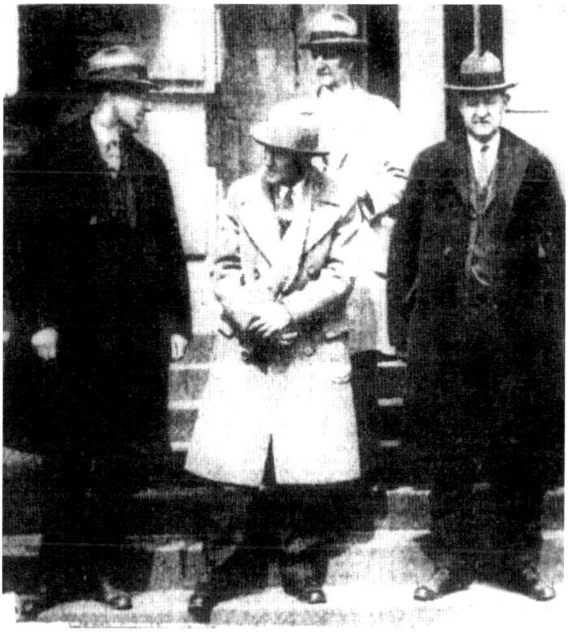

As seen in the *Lake County Times* of April 22, 1926, Dan Hesly (*center foreground*) leaves the federal courthouse at Hammond in the company of postal inspectors and a U.S. marshal. *Author's collection.*

Hostert responded, "Yes, sir, I am positive that that man is the man who shot Mr. Fisher." The Mokenian also interjected that Hesly's knees visibly shook when he saw Dr. McMahan at the lineup—to him a clear indication of guilt. When they saw him at Crown Point, the doctor himself said, "That is absolutely the man that stole my car" in reference to the theft that ultimately led to Deputy Fisher's death.

As the case against Dan Hesly was building, the detectives who had moved him to Crown Point told the media that he had become very morose at the gravity of the whole situation, especially when it became clear that the Illinois authorities were looking to pin Fisher's murder on him. Even though he emphatically denied having anything to do with the officer's killing, Hesly could sense which direction the events were taking. With a resigned air, he told the *Lake County Times*, "My life is over now."[103]

CHAPTER 13

A QUESTION OF GUILT

As Dan Hesly languished in the jail at Crown Point, Indiana, he not only awaited trial on robbery charges but also found himself at the end of pointed fingers accusing him of being Walter Fisher's killer. From the readers' vantage point over ninety years after the fact, we are confronted with a painful dearth of extant forensic evidence and other records; therefore, we can't see exactly what it was that tipped the scales for the investigators, what drew their investigative focus away from Santo Calabrese and onto Hesly. Past the end of April 1926, all previous mentions of Calabrese having been not only Fisher's assailant but also the Indiana Harbor thief are sanitized out of the narrative, and going into the future, they seem to have been never fully acknowledged. This switch in suspects hugely complicates the entire story. In response to the initial chaos of the case that came with Hesly's arrest, authorities admitted to purposely spinning a complex web of deception that it fed to the media. Looking back, historians will never know whether this was true or if Chicago-area law enforcement and postal inspectors were saving face for having falsely identified Calabrese as the thief and killer.

If one assumes that investigators and media had it all right and that Dan Hesly alone executed the Indiana Harbor heist and later shot and killed Deputy Walter Fisher, there's no getting around certain issues. The heaviest evidence against Hesly seems to be eyewitness testimony, namely that Barney Hostert and Dr. Ernest McMahan were positive that he was the man they encountered on April 14. However, their identifications didn't come until much later, not until the other, original man they fingered was literally dead and buried. Eyewitness testimony is notoriously unreliable, and it shouldn't be overlooked that the Mokenians could have easily been under duress when they viewed Hesly in the lineup. During Fisher's inquest, Hostert would testify that his glimpse of the killer was fleeting, stating, "I just got a flash," almost as if to downplay his ability to properly identify any shooter. Not only that, but upon first viewing Calabrese's bloody body at the Speedway Hospital, Hostert would only commit to the fact that his clothes were close to what he remembered the shooter wearing.

Another unavoidable facet of the case is the time it allegedly took Hesly to make the trip from Joliet, where he ditched Frank Watson and his car at the Ridgewood Service Station, to the Cleveland farm outside Mokena, where Dr. McMahan's Ford was stolen. For Hesly to have covered this distance on foot, one of nearly eight miles, between roughly 10:00 and 10:30 a.m. that morning would have required superhuman speed. The Mokena *News-Bulletin* led the charge in terms of questioning this time frame, asserting that "it was impossible for Hesley [*sic*], in the short time after he left the garage until the killing of Fisher, to reach the spot where the latter was killed." It is known that investigators explored the possibility that Hesly could have hitched another ride between the garage and the spot outside Mokena, but it never panned out.

On the same note, it's an established fact that Deputy Fisher, as he himself was being shot, was able to return fire. It is extremely likely that at least some of his rounds found their mark, and for this, we need not rely solely on the testimony of Barney Hostert. When Dr. McMahan's car was found later that day near Melrose Park, the machine was pierced by bullet holes and contained copious splatters of blood. Most damningly, when Dan Hesly was arrested a week after the shooting, he displayed no signs of having been recently shot. At the continuation of the inquests on April 30, Hostert was specifically asked if he knew of any bullet wounds on Hesly's person when he was seen at the lineup in Crown Point. His response was a definite no, testifying, "No sign of a bullet, not that they told us." That day, Hesly only had a gash on the left side of his face that was supposed to have been caused by glass.

Once again, we come to Deputy Fisher and his frenzied fire back at his attacker. Aside from a shot to the skull that killed Santo Calabrese, he also sustained two superficial wounds in his hand and back. Numerous media sources, along with the inquest records, mention that the non-mortal wounds were sourced by a different caliber of round than that which caused the fatal head wound. In reference to the gunshot wounds, the *Chicago Daily News* stated that, according to police, "Fisher probably hit him before he himself was killed," while the *Daily Tribune* said that "three [*sic*] of the shots are supposed to have been fired by Fisher."[104] Taking a much more definitive stance, the *Joliet Evening Herald-News* printed that "Calabrese was wounded in the back and the hand by bullets of the same size as those used by Fisher."[105] The presence of these extra wounds suffered by Calabrese led law enforcement figures early in the investigation to construct what appeared to them to be the likely scenario behind his fate. Before the shift in analytical attention to Hesly, the working theory making the media rounds was that Calabrese himself was the perpetrator of the Indiana Harbor heist, and after escaping from Joliet and stealing Dr. McMahan's car outside Mokena, he shot Walter Fisher near Orland, only afterward to be betrayed by unnamed co-conspirators who killed him for the loot.

The experience of Frank Watson must also be taken into consideration. The driver who transported the payroll of Inland Steel on the morning of April 14 was unfortunate enough to be in the presence of the hijacker during their forced journey from Indiana Harbor to Joliet. Upon being shown Santo Calabrese's body less than a day later, Watson was firm in his belief that this man was not his kidnapper.[106] He would go as far as saying that Calabrese might have looked like his captor but that he wasn't the same man. Watson's statement lends credence to the theory that Hesly was the Indiana Harbor robber but not the man who attacked Walter Fisher.

Let the reader temporarily put Dan Hesly and his pronounced guilt in Fisher's murder aside and instead conclude that Santo Calabrese was the deputy's killer. Parting the fog of time, we realize that whoever murdered the deputy was almost surely also shot in the exchange, due to the proximity in which they fired at each other. Not only did Barney Hostert testify to this extent, but a trail of blood was found at the scene near Orland, and more blood was later found in Dr. McMahan's car once it was recovered later that day.

Inferring that Santo Calabrese was the actual killer, more questions flood to the forefront. What was he doing in that spot outside Mokena, a place he seemingly had no connection to, on the morning of April 14 when he carjacked Dr. McMahan? From what or whom was he fleeing? Did Calabrese have any connection whatsoever to the earlier events of the day, the Indiana Harbor heist? Despite these details and the question of whether he truly fits into this narrative, Santo Calabrese tangled with the wrong people, and he paid dearly. Once again, the troublesome lack of investigative peculiars that have survived the decades make an uncomfortable amount of this case's facets hard to clarify.

Santo Calabrese was never given his day in court, having been brutally murdered before his innocence or guilt could be proven. Therefore, in the absence of so much concrete, smoking gun evidence in this case, it is unfair to label him the murderer of Walter Fisher once and for all. However, most of what survives heavily points to him. A few succinct lines that *News-Bulletin* editor William Semmler printed in the aftermath of Fisher's untimely death sum up everything the best: "Regardless of the fact who the murderer is, the cold fact remains that Walter Fisher is dead, his wife a widow and his children fatherless—and all for what?"[107]

CHAPTER 14

THE IRON DOOR

It was time for the swift hammer of justice to land on Dan Hesly. On Wednesday afternoon, May 26, 1926, a federal grand jury convening in Indianapolis indicted him for the $37,000 heist in Indiana Harbor.[108] The charge officially laid the responsibility at his feet for the kidnapping of driver Frank Watson and for his transport over the Illinois border with the cash loot to Joliet, where his escape fell apart. Since Hesly packed a gun during the robbery, he found himself facing a steep prison sentence of at least twenty-five years. While trying to seek peace with the government, his lawyer tried to file a guilty plea to a lesser charge of larceny of the mails,[109] which carried a lighter sentence. When federal judge Thomas Slick refused to take it, in a last-ditch effort to escape decades behind bars, Hesly pleaded not guilty.

The trial was held on July 6, 1926, at Judge Slick's federal court in Hammond,[110] about six miles from the scene of the crime in Indiana Harbor. In addition to the standard court personnel in attendance, Helen Hesly was also there that day, cradling her and Dan's month-old daughter, Lorraine. In tow with Hesly was his attorney, A.J. Muffoletto of Chicago, who lodged a guilty plea for his client, reflecting a complete turnaround of his earlier stance. Covering the proceedings, the *Lake County Star* cynically noted that they were "as devoid of the spectacular as the actual robbery was replete with the sensational."[111] It was a rudimentary process, one completely by the books. U.S. district attorney of Indianapolis Albert Ward went through the details of the case, including the timeline of the caper and the particulars of Hesly's capture.

Judge Slick didn't need long to decide the defendant's guilt or innocence, his mind being made up twelve minutes after the arraignment. At the end of the trial at two o'clock, his gavel sounded, and Dan Hesly was slapped with a sentence of twenty-five years, to be served behind the towering walls of the federal prison at Leavenworth, Kansas. He was turned over to two United States marshals tasked with transporting him there the following morning.

Before the robbery trial had even started that summer, a far more serious charge against Dan Hesly was already in the works. At the end of April, as he sat in the Lake County Jail at Crown Point, Indiana, a grand jury in Chicago indicted him for the murder of Walter Fisher.[112] An allegation that had previously only been relegated to speculation in the law enforcement community was now official. Barely settled in at Leavenworth, Hesly was hauled back to his hometown the following spring to stand the murder charge in yet another trial. On April 10, 1927, almost exactly a year to the day after Deputy Fisher's death, Dan Hesly was delivered to Chicago authorities under a writ of habeas corpus, and the murder trial started on April 18 under Judge Philip L. Sullivan. The judge was known to bristle at the thought of criminal trials that stretched on seemingly without end and, in the words of the *Chicago Tribune*, had "gradually tightened up on the latitude allowed attorneys in jury selecting, especially in murder cases."[113] Judge Sullivan picked the jurors himself and breezed through it in less than two days, in a time and place when it wasn't unheard of for the process to drag on for weeks. Those the judge wound up selecting were veniremen from a typical cross-section of the population, among them a bookkeeper, a secretary, a plant superintendent and a clerk for a railroad company.[114] As her husband's fate was about to be decided yet again, Helen Hesly was present during jury selection along with baby Lorraine.

Assistant State's Attorneys Emmet Byrne and Frank Matousek sought nothing less than the highest possible punishment for the ex-athlete. They planned to ask for the death penalty, and in light thereof, Dan Hesly was defiant of the charge against him and emphatically declared himself not guilty. The day the trial started, he scoffed at the allegation and, speaking freely, told the *Tribune*, "They can't connect me with the killing" and, repeating a common trope of the case, went on to say that "it was impossible for me to have been at the scene of the shooting near Orland. At the time I was stalled in Joliet."[115] During the proceedings, Hesly was quiet, didn't put up much of a defense and was under the watchful eyes of a special contingent of guards who had come from Leavenworth. He did not take the stand, as court attachés would later say that doing so would have

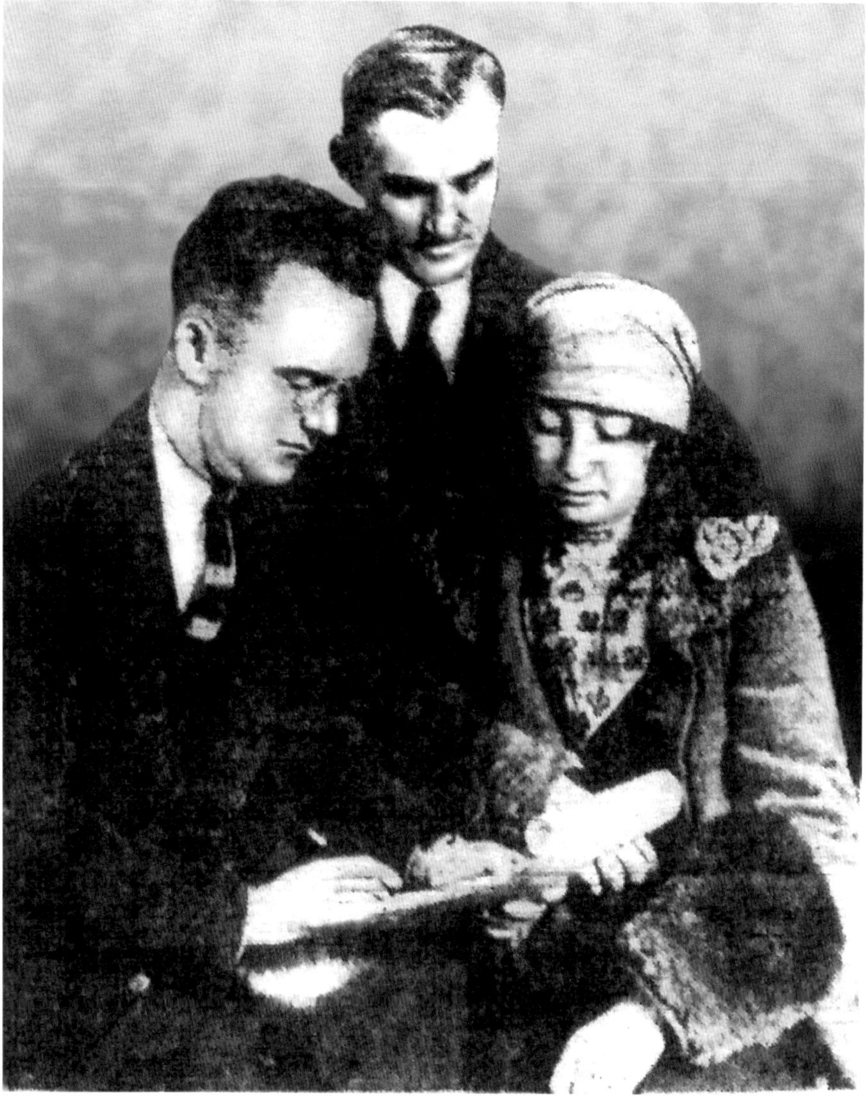

Deputy Fisher's widow, Ethel Fisher, pictured by the *Chicago Daily Journal* with assistant state's attorneys Emmet Byrne (*left*) and Frank Matousek (*center*) during Dan Hesly's murder trial. *Author's collection.*

put him at great risk to the state's withering cross-examination. Mokena resident Ethel Fisher, widow of the fallen deputy, gave her testimony on April 20, and the following day, her fellow townsman Dr. Ernest McMahan recounted for the umpteenth time the story of how his vehicle had been stolen from under him outside town the year before and how this act set into motion the events leading to Walter Fisher's death.[116]

On April 21, 1927, the jurors reached a verdict of guilty and passed down to Dan Hesly a sentence of twenty-five years for Walter Fisher's murder. It remains unclear exactly what evidence they heard in the case and what ultimately convinced them of his guilt. Perhaps most importantly, at this late date it's ambiguous why they spared him the hangman's noose. The term was set to be carried out at the Illinois State Penitentiary in Joliet, the scene of the mail robbery's collapse, after the rest of his twenty-five-year sentence for that crime was finished at Leavenworth.

Once the verdict was in, Judge Sullivan was furious. To the press, he openly referred to it as a travesty of justice and later in his chambers was quoted by the *Tribune* as saying that "this case justifies…either a sentence of hanging, or at least life imprisonment. There is no doubt in my mind but that Hesley [*sic*] killed the deputy sheriff in cold blood while seeking to escape after he had committed the mail robbery and held up a physician for his automobile."[117] Assistant State's Attorney Byrne was also flummoxed and wondered aloud "what juries want in the way of evidence." While later reflecting on the defendant's past criminal record and the Indiana Harbor heist, he told the jurors in a mystified manner after the trial that "any one of his robbery crimes [would] carry a penalty of from ten years to life, yet you give him only a twenty-five-year sentence for the murder." Byrne and his prosecutorial colleague Matousek pessimistically noted that if Hesly kept up good behavior behind bars, neither sentence would equal close to the half century allotted. In the eyes of the law, Dan Hesly was the triggerman who took Walter Fisher's life. Regardless of whether he actually was or not, he was going to pay.

CHAPTER 15

THE PATH TO REHABILITATION

So it was that Daniel Hesly, inmate number 25729, was sent to the United States Penitentiary at Leavenworth, Kansas, a large civilian facility that is often confused with the military prison on the nearby Fort Leavenworth army base. Little has survived the ravages of time as to what Hesly's life was like at this institution, although his wife, Helen, divorced him around three years after he entered the penal system. Eight years after the verdict in the Indiana Harbor mail robbery case, Dan was first eligible for parole on November 8, 1934. In the words of a later progress report, he "declined to file" and stayed at Leavenworth. While incarcerated in Kansas, he returned to his old area of passion and expertise: the radio. He found work in the prison's electric shop and radio booth, where pen bureaucrats noted that he performed exemplary work.

At Leavenworth, Dan Hesly racked up a handful of institutional rule violations. Soon after his arrival, he was reprimanded for wasting food, and in May 1927, he was found to have an oil can and cooking cocoa in his possession but wasn't punished, as he, in the words of a disciplinary report, "had nothing to do with the matter." On June 30, 1931, it was noted that he and "four others were engaged in a free for all fight on the balcony of [the] main chapel." Years later, Hesly would describe the incident, noting that one of his fellow prisoners was "assaulted with an iron bar by an inmate....As the victim was knocked down, the assaulting person continued to beat my co-worker. It was my duty to step in and stop what I believe would eventually have been murder, as no guard was present." Somewhat

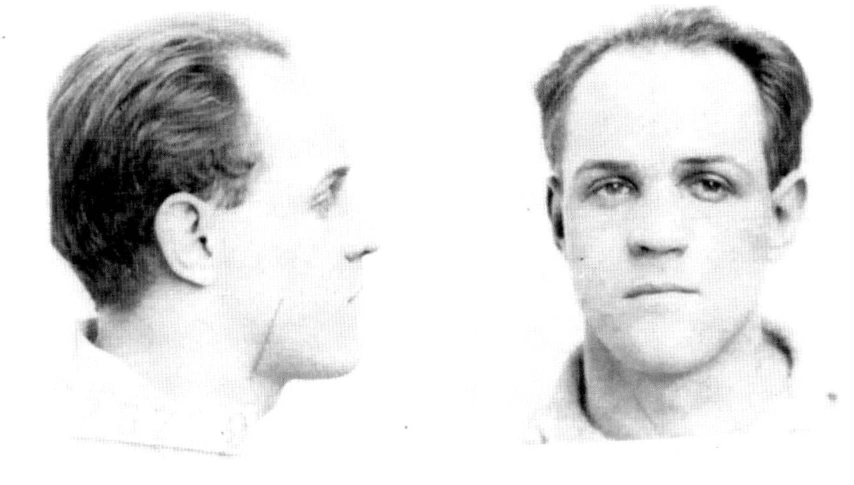

Dan Hesly around the time he began his twenty-five-year sentence for mail robbery at the United States Penitentiary at Leavenworth, Kansas. *Courtesy National Archives.*

sarcastically summing up the incident, he would write, "Apparently saving a life constitutes fighting."[118]

In spite of these incidents, Hesly went through various strikes and even the riot of 1929 at Leavenworth without having any part in them. In 1936, a glaring mark was entered on his record that had a profound effect on this course of his rehabilitation. In terms of official reports, very little details on the exact occurrence were noted for posterity, other than that prisoner Hesly was transferred to a type of segregation unit at Leavenworth on the grounds of "sex tendencies," namely for a vaguely defined "act of degeneracy" with an inmate named Parton that happened on September 14, 1935. In subsequent interviews with authorities, Hesly would do his best to play down the incident and would even claim that it was a misunderstanding involving a rule violation of having another inmate in his cell. Years down the line, he would write that "this report was evidently interpreted with a vivid imagination." Defending himself in the later account, Hesly wrote, "Every official that knows me realized that the intimated character does not fit my personality." The whole episode happened when Dan was managing an inmate baseball team, on which Parton was a pitcher. After having strained his arm and back, the player came to Hesly's cell, where Dan "rubbed him down with liniment." He also noted that "most ball players are prima donnas and have to be given considerable care." The incident took place in the cell to, in Dan's words, "avoid encounters as experienced previously with the degenerate negro orderlies assigned to the parole room. They had repeatedly tried to seduce this boy by offering home brew as an inducement to come to their rooms." In a report written years later, a prison official would note with a resigned attitude that there were not many surviving details of the episode and that inmate Hesly "has always indignantly denied it." The same administrator reported "that he should be given the benefit of the doubt" in regard to the entire incident.

Regardless of what transpired in September 1935, prison authorities were anxious to get Hesly out of Leavenworth due to the incident, and thus it transpired that Dan Hesly was relocated to the San Francisco Bay in California, where on September 25, 1936, federal inmate number 343 was processed into the federal penitentiary at Alcatraz. While behind bars on "the Rock," Hesly's prison life was quiet; he abided by the rules and didn't cause trouble for others or himself. There are only two disciplinary infractions recorded in his prison reports, both of which were relatively minor and for which no harsh punishment was dealt. On an August morning in 1938, without any complaint or explanation, he left a serving of applesauce untouched on his breakfast tray. In response, his noon lunch was forfeited later that day. Less than a year later in March 1939, Junior Officer C.Y. Hurst reported Hesly for loudly laughing and talking in the mess hall. For this, he was simply reprimanded and warned against repeating such behavior.

While locked up on Alcatraz, Hesly worked in this institution's laundry, where his overseers noted that he was very industrious and a good worker, having stayed on the job even during the great strike of 1937. He made good use of his time behind bars and completed correspondence courses from the University of California, one in advanced English grammar that was somewhat difficult for him, while his course in advanced shop mathematics came much more easily. Hesly also took lessons in astronomy and diesel work. In a 1939 health interview with psychiatrist Romney M. Ritchey, his intellectual development was shown to be above average, and it was noted that he was "alert and observing and wants to be friendly," where at the beginning of the talk, he came across as being clammed up. During the conversation, Dan Hesly raised the interesting point that he felt neglected due to the stigma under which he arrived at Alcatraz and that, in his opinion, the original case back at Leavenworth hadn't been given proper diligence or he wouldn't have been transferred to California. It was left unnoted whether

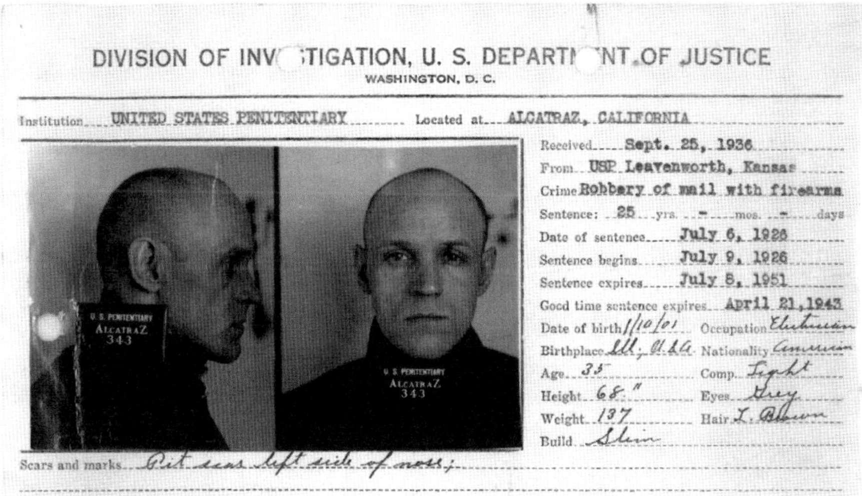

DIVISION OF INVESTIGATION, U. S. DEPARTMENT OF JUSTICE
WASHINGTON, D. C.

Institution UNITED STATES PENITENTIARY Located at ALCATRAZ, CALIFORNIA

U. S. PENITENTIARY ALCATRAZ 343

Received Sept. 25, 1936
From USP Leavenworth, Kansas
Crime Robbery of mail with firearms
Sentence: 25 yrs. - mos. - days
Date of sentence July 6, 1926
Sentence begins July 9, 1926
Sentence expires July 8, 1951
Good time sentence expires April 21, 1943
Date of birth 1/10/01 Occupation Electrician
Birthplace Ill., U.S.A. Nationality American
Age 35 Comp. Light
Height 68" Eyes Grey
Weight 137 Hair L. Brown
Build Slim
Scars and marks Pit scar left side of nose;

Logging personal details down to his scars, this card was completed along with Dan Hesly's mug shot upon his arrival at Alcatraz. *Courtesy National Archives.*

these matters were followed up on. Dr. Ritchey didn't consider Dan to be psychotic but noted him to be emotionally unstable and impulsive in conduct.

In an application for executive clemency dated May 23, 1938, Hesly asked for a commutation of his sentence.[119] Completed on Alcatraz with perfect penmanship and a smoothly flowing narrative, the forms provide a vivid window into Dan Hesly's mind, one that was frustrated with numerous aspects of his incarceration yet also proud of his accomplishments behind bars. In his application, he laid out his history as a convict, beginning with the fact that he complied with Chief Post Office Inspector Grant B. Miller's wishes in the aftermath of his arrest for the Indiana Harbor heist back in 1926, namely to "make good the money taken in the robbery, reveal my source of information, [and] enter a plea of guilty to obliterate the necessity of an expensive trial." Hesly reminded the reader that all the conditions were met, but "twelve years have passed without consideration for… clemency." He also highlighted his various achievements, among which were assisting in civil engineering and "estimating of materials" that went into the construction of two hospital annexes and a storeroom that were built in 1927 at Leavenworth; the drawing of plans for a furniture factory and guard towers that went through only "a few minor changes" by an army engineer before being implemented; and the completion of detailed drawings for a brochure during the Hoover administration.

The petitioner also emphasized his deeds with radio work at the aforementioned prison, including his work designing and installing a "centralized radio installation," which he claimed was the world's largest, while in 1933, an RCA representative working with Hesly on another project was so impressed by his skills that he was offered "employment at the time I should be released from prison." With no small amount of bravado, Dan wrote, "I cite these accomplishments to show that I have gained an excellent education and moulded [*sic*] a character that is very antagonistic towards a life of crime. The work accomplished and education acquired is undoubtedly the most exceptional case in the history of federal prisons."

Hesly also addressed his disciplinary history, and some bad blood came up. In the margin of his letter, Dan penciled "I don't get it," while he noted that he had "encountered the many rules which are necessary for the operation of an institution, but nevertheless petty." He noted that the old fighting incident at Leavenworth "should at least warrant a compliment, instead of a reprimand" due to his having saved a man's life, at least from his own point of view. In reference to the incident of alleged "degeneracy" that earned him the trip to Alcatraz, he noted that the "report is nothing but a heinous intimation." In reading the application, it becomes clear that Hesly was looking to start serving his twenty-five-year sentence for the murder of Deputy Fisher, as he knew that his eventual transfer to the Illinois State Penitentiary at Joliet would allow his parents to visit him. In an especially touching passage, Hesly penned, "My folks are near 80 years old. I have not seen them for ten years. I beg of you, for their sake, that I may see them before they pass to the great beyond."

As to the results of this plea for clemency, Hesly doesn't appear to have received any leniency toward his sentence for the mail robbery. In the spring of 1942, as the country was barely a year into the Second World War, he found himself transferred out of Alcatraz and back to the United States Penitentiary in Leavenworth, Kansas. As is the case with so many of the details pertaining to his time behind bars, the exact reason behind the move was never recorded. Dan barely did any time there during his second stint in Kansas before he was finally sent back to his home state of Illinois to begin doing time for the murder of Deputy Fisher sixteen years before. He was reported present at the Cook County Jail in Chicago on August 16, 1942, and eleven days later on August 27, Hesly arrived at the Illinois State Penitentiary at Joliet, where he was processed in as inmate number 19390. Located about two and a half miles from the site of the Ridgewood Service Station, where everything during his escape from the Indiana Harbor heist

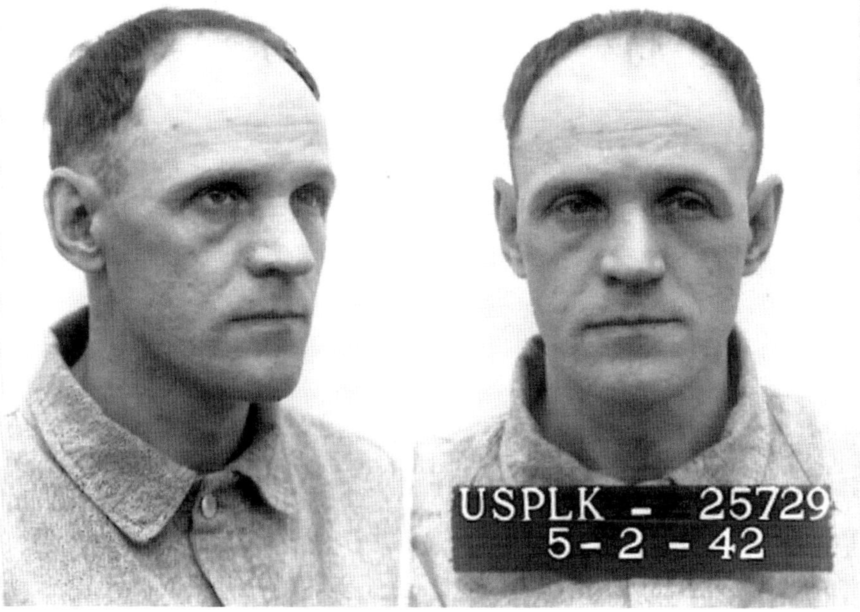

A dour Dan Hesly is pictured here in 1942, the sixteenth year of his imprisonment. *Courtesy National Archives.*

started going south, the facility could easily have been mistaken for a medieval castle with its high stone walls and turreted watchtowers. First opened in 1858, prior to Hesly's arrival the prison had housed such infamous inmates as Chicago gangster George "Bugs" Moran and murderers Nathan Leopold and Richard Loeb. Per the pattern, another vital piece of information is missing in this period of Hesly's life—namely, the date of his release from Joliet. The nearest bit of data that has survived indicates that around 1954, Dan Hesly was let out from behind the iron door and lived the rest of his life as a free man.

CHAPTER 16

FREEDOM'S GATE

A little girl named Dottie was five years old on Thanksgiving 1955 when her mother invited a guest to join them for their holiday dinner. She beheld him and was impressed by the dignified way in which he carried himself, not to mention his suit and general sense of cleanliness. Dan Hesly met Dottie's mother, Rose Taglia, a professional dancer and seamstress, at Chicago's Aragon Ballroom, and the two were married on December 6, 1956. Over the years, Dottie would grow very close to her stepfather, who treated her with the love and affection afforded to his own flesh and blood. He encouraged out-of-the-box ideas and fostered philosophical thought. He loved to play solitaire, which Dottie would later attribute to his years spent behind bars, and was known to have a temper but never turned violent.

Possessed of a mind for the technical side of things, after his release from prison, Hesly went on to become an industrial electrician, a career he flourished in for thirty years. He finally retired around 1978, after which he and Rose lived in Florida for a period before ultimately resettling in McHenry County, northwest of Chicago. Law-abiding and respected by those who knew him, Dan Hesly was a man who didn't rock the boat and preferred to stay off the radar. Nevertheless, while a Florida resident, he was involved in a foreboding incident involving a judge with whom he had come into acquaintance. The judge confronted Hesly and warned him with the stern statement that Hesly's past was known to him and he'd better watch his back. This exchange only heightened the general distrust of law enforcement figures that Dan had developed over the years, which also played out in his displeasure at Dottie's having worked as a parole officer in the 1980s.

As an elderly man in July 1986, Dan found himself in a car accident that resulted in a nasty bump on the head. He was never quite the same after the wreck and underwent a profound change afterward. By this time in their lives, his stepdaughter Dottie had become well aware of his criminal past and the details behind his long conviction. In the sunset of his life, even after most of his mental facilities had deteriorated, Dan continued insisting to her that he had never shot anyone aside from himself, in reference to the incident that took place during his alleged army service.

Dan Hesly breathed his last on March 19, 1991, in Woodstock, Illinois. He far outlived every other principal player from those dark days in 1926, and any secrets regarding the murder of Walter Fisher and the Indiana Harbor heist were taken with him to the grave. It bears noting that almost twenty years after his death, Hesly's stepdaughter Dottie recounted to this author a very interesting story in this regard. According to her, in years past, Dan had clued her in to some facts behind the 1926 robbery. In his words, it resulted from the fact that he was deeply in debt to a Chicago underworld figure who had lent him money to finance a radio-related venture. As the story went, the original lender disappeared, and his replacement threatened bodily harm on Hesly's pregnant wife, Helen, which led to the stick-up to repay him. The man who shot Deputy Fisher had been waiting to accept the loot in Joliet but panicked when Dan never showed after his auto broke down and caused the chase with Fisher and Barney Hostert after stealing Dr. McMahan's car near Mokena. This story is within the realm of possibility, makes sense and is indeed very compelling, but nevertheless, at this late date there is no way to verify any of it, and it must be regarded as apocryphal.

CHAPTER 17

SETTLING DUST

No one was ever prosecuted for the murder of Santo Calabrese. Quickly forgotten in a time and place where violence was a way of life, his death is included as another nameless hash mark in the tally of seventy-five gangland killings in and around Chicago during 1926.[120] His wife, Concetta, whose name surfaced almost as a whisper on his death certificate, quickly faded into the background of history.

Dr. Ernest G. McMahan, whose Ford coupe was jacked near the Cleveland farm on April 14, 1926, and set into action a disastrous chain of events, practiced medicine in Mokena until at least the mid-1950s. By the time he ultimately left town, he had come to serve on the executive committee of Silver Cross Hospital in Joliet[121] and also taught at its school of nursing. Many of his former patients in the village still affectionately remember him as "Doc." He spent his final days in Texas, where he passed away an elderly man in December 1978.[122]

Barney Hostert stayed in Mokena and with his Ford agency for the rest of his days. From the day of the shooting onward, he carried a visible scar from the shard of glass that nicked his face when the bullets flew. At Walter Fisher's inquest, it was recorded as having been on his forehead, but those who knew him say it was on his nose. As the years marched on, Barney was reticent to talk about the incident; one usually had to pump him for details. If anything was said, he often resorted to a kind of gallows humor to lighten the situation; on at least one occasion, he dismissively said that "I should have put my boots on a little slower that day." Barney Hostert died on December 11, 1959, having reached sixty-eight years.[123]

After Walter Fisher's murder, Mokena police chief John Frisch wasn't long for the force. The man who fought crime in town side by side with Walter threw down his star and quit during a volatile village board meeting not quite eight months after Walter's death, the heart of the matter being an issue with the community water tower. After his tenure as village constable, he devoted his energy full time to railroad work. He lived until March 1932, when he lost his life to an infection.[124]

The dark veil of tragedy hung tightly on the Fisher family after Walter's death. Within a few months, his wife, Ethel, had leased his store to the A&P Tea Company, which wound up remodeling the place.[125] She also kept a small dry goods and shoe store adjoining it,[126] but the business didn't last very long. By 1930, she had moved back to her hometown of Joliet with her daughters and was working there as a beautician in her own shop. In February 1931, Ethel contracted pulmonary tuberculosis, and she lost her battle with it on September 13, 1931, at the Chicago Presbyterian Hospital,[127] sometimes also referred to as the Chicago Fresh Air Hospital. Like her husband, Ethel Fisher had died tragically young, passing away at the age of thirty-three. Numerous old friends and neighbors from Mokena attended her funeral in Joliet on September 14, her burial taking place within twenty-four hours of her death, in accordance with Jewish tradition. Ethel was interred at Mount Moriah Cemetery at the county seat, under a headstone that matched her late husband's.

At the time of their mother's death, Lucille and Rosalyn Fisher were thirteen and eleven years old, respectively, effectively orphans who would go on to spend time in institutions and foster homes. Lucille eventually married a man named Kaufman and, around 1940, moved to Detroit, where she settled down and raised a daughter. She died there of an unspecified illness on January 20, 1952, just short of her thirty-fourth birthday.[128] Even though she hadn't lived in Mokena since her childhood, word of her death reached town, and her passing was noted on the front page of the *News-Bulletin*, the same small-town paper that so movingly memorialized her father back in

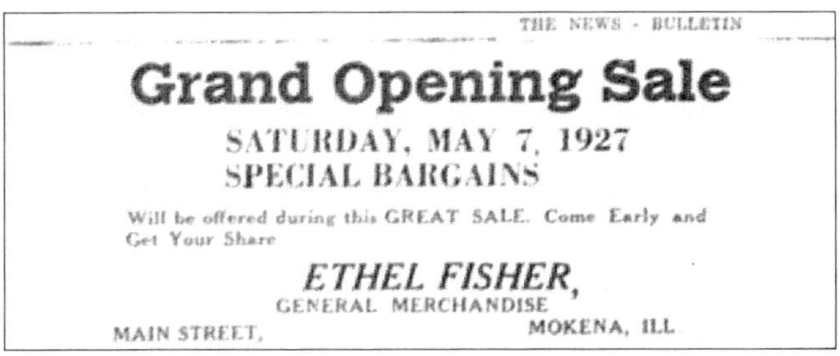

On May 6, 1927, the *News-Bulletin* ran this ad announcing the opening of Ethel Fisher's store on Mokena's Front Street. *Author's collection.*

'26. In a powerfully reminiscent way, the melancholy story of his demise was tacked onto his daughter's obituary. Lucille Kaufman was buried next to her mother at Mount Moriah Cemetery in Joliet.

Rosalyn Fisher outlived them all by far. She would go on to marry Charles Jones and build a career as a nurse and, by the 1990s, was calling Maricopa County, Arizona home. At the end of that decade, word reached Rosalyn that a memorial was being erected in Joliet, the city of her birth, to remember the fallen law enforcement officers of Will County. Her father's name was to be etched with thirty others in granite on a monument in front of the Will County courthouse. Rosalyn was filled with pride that his sacrifice would be ennobled at the shrine, which was built entirely by locally raised contributions—$100 of which came from Rosalyn herself.[129] In a letter that came with her donation, she wrote, "It's wonderful that I can contribute something to my father, I remember so very little about him." At the time of the letter, she was living in an Arizona hospice unit suffering from cancer. The unveiling of the monument took place on May 9, 1999, but it came too late for Rosalyn Jones, who had crossed the great beyond only five days before on May 4.[130]

Orland Park, whose outskirts bore witness to Walter Fisher's killing in the spring of 1926, was at the time a sleepy farming hamlet. After the Second World War, the town experienced unprecedented growth and, as of this writing, is the premier community of south Chicagoland. Structures that were around in the 1920s are as rare as the proverbial hen's teeth, although time has spared Dr. Schussler's office, where Walter breathed his last, the house looking much the same today as it did then. The same cannot be said for the intersection where the fatal shooting took place, which is now the home of some of the greater suburban area's leading residential and retail property. It would be wholly unrecognizable to those who were there on April 14.

Just down the road and to the south is Mokena, the old home of the Fishers and most of the other principal players in this narrative. While not quite on the scale of Orland Park, this village also experienced a boom after the war, which unfortunately carried with it the loss of many of the landmarks that would have been familiar to those players. The historic building that housed Walter Fisher's store is long gone, having burned in an as-yet unexplained blaze in the fall of 1929,[131] the last physical vestige of his time in Mokena gone barely three years after his death. The collective memories of Walter's murder have become muddled by time and age. When the author first became familiar with the grander scheme of the community's history, the episode of Walter Fisher's killing was foggily remembered as having taken

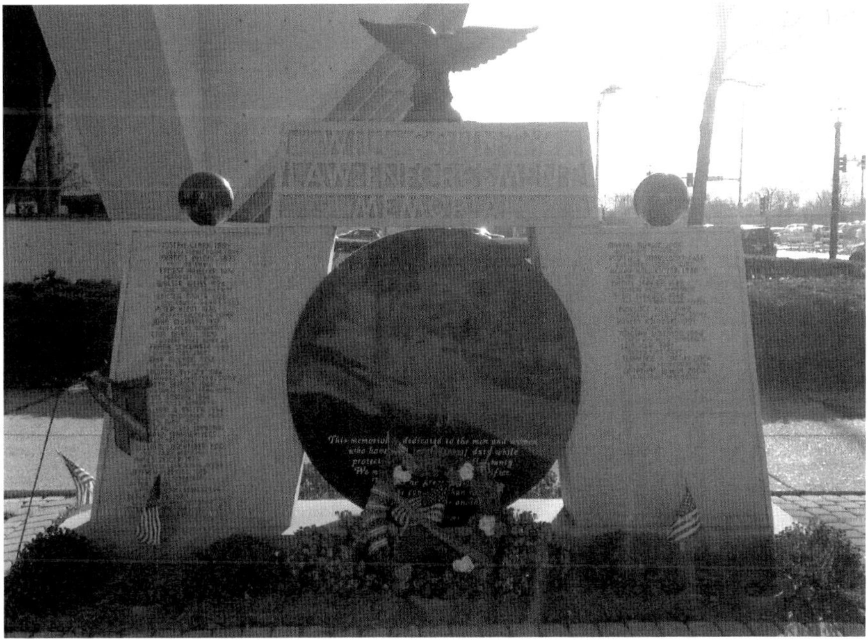

Dedicated in 1999, this monument honors the fallen law enforcement officers of Will County, Illinois. It stands on the courthouse lawn in Joliet. *Author's collection.*

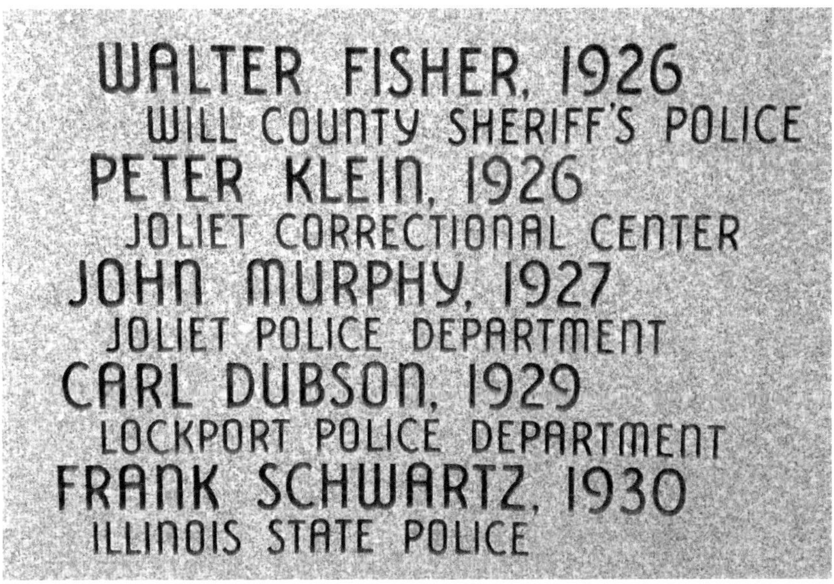

The Will County Law Enforcement memorial enshrines the names of thirty fallen officers, including that of Walter Fisher. *Author's collection.*

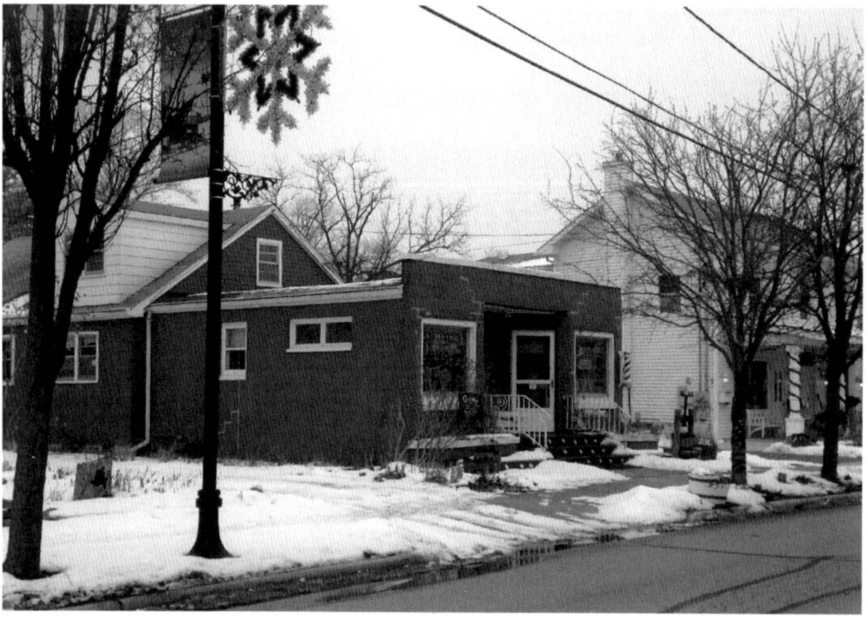

No trace remains of the historic building where Walter Fisher lived and worked in Mokena, it having been lost in a fire in 1929. This structure currently stands at today's 11014 Front Street. *Author's collection.*

place in a car chase with the robbers of the Mokena State Bank in October 1924; so it has come to be falsely recalled by a small handful of residents. Although both events occurred separately as well as a year and a half apart, over the years, these two major crimes of the decade in question have become amalgamated in the cumulative remembrance.

While he sways over the village like a silent ghost, Walter Fisher's name is conspicuously absent in the Mokena of today. His dedication to his home was paid for in his blood, and this ultimate sacrifice has been completely forgotten. While his name is inscribed with others on the courthouse lawn monument in Joliet, no memorial stands in his hometown, no park or street or even a bench bears his name. On April 14, 1926, an epic robbery befell the faceless Inland Steel Company, one that inconvenienced the concern but one from which it ultimately bounced back, richer than ever. That day, a life was also brutally robbed, and Walter Fisher's family was forced to go down a long and painful road without him. He gave his life protecting his community, his neighbors and their property. In the words of editor William Semmler of the Mokena *News-Bulletin*, "He was a real hero in every sense of the word and this community should always revere his memory."[132]

A WORD ON SOURCES

Newspapers from all over the country picked up the story of the Indiana Harbor robbery and the subsequent murder of Walter Fisher. No conversational details or any other aspects of this chronicle have had any artistic license applied to them; every fact is presented exactly as it was recorded. Naturally, in detailing a historic event separated from the author by many decades, certain difficulties did arise. Tracing the exact route of Walter Fisher and Barney Hostert in their pursuit of the thief of Dr. Ernest McMahan's auto between Mokena and Orland Park remains problematic, as many of the country roads traversed weren't called by their proper names in surviving accounts or lacked names altogether. Luckily, the journalistic record as well as other documents have remained clear as to precisely where the fatal shooting took place.

The courtroom transcripts of Fisher's murder trial were unfortunately and perhaps unwisely destroyed years ago, although luckily the testimony from the Cook County coroner's inquests of both Santo Calabrese and Walter Fisher have completely survived and have proven to be rich, irreplaceable pieces of historic evidence, as key witnesses like Hostert and Dr. McMahan were grilled repeatedly by investigators. These interrogations have allowed the two men's accounts to be recorded in unprecedented detail.

NOTES

Chapter 1

1. Rose Keefe, *The Man Who Got Away: The Bugs Moran Story: A Biography* (Nashville, TN: Cumberland House, 2005).
2. "Suspicious Gents Call at Mokena Telephone Office," *News-Bulletin*, November 10, 1922.
3. "Underground Brewery Has Real Old Time Beer," *News-Bulletin*, August 28, 1924.
4. "Will County Deputies Raid Mokena Alderman's Saloon; Seize Moonshine, Punch Board," *News-Bulletin*, January 23, 1925.
5. "U.S. Probes Mokena Beer Shipment," *News-Bulletin*, August 18, 1922.
6. "Mysterious Shots Fired at Mokena Jail," *News-Bulletin*, April 14, 1922.
7. "Four Men with Drawn Guns Force Henry Yunker of Mokena to Hitch Up Horse and Pull Auto out of Mud," *News-Bulletin*, April 4, 1924.
8. "Negroes Hold Up Orland Post Office and Shoot at Postmaster Schmaedeke; Make Escape," *News-Bulletin*, October 12, 1923.
9. "Mokena Bank Held Up," *News-Bulletin*, October 30, 1924.

Chapter 2

10. 1920 Federal Census of Village of Mokena, Frankfort Township, Will County, Illinois.

11. World War I Draft Registration Card 706, dated September 12, 1918.
12. 1910 Federal Census of Louisville City, Ward 5, Jefferson County, Kentucky.
13. Will County Marriage Certificate #32748.
14. 1900 Federal Census of Joliet Township, Will County, Illinois.
15. *Gleanings and Biographies* (n.p.: Will County Historical Society, 1969).
16. *News-Bulletin*, February 10, 1922.
17. Ibid., March 10, 1922.
18. Ibid., April 6, 1923.
19. Ibid., August 4, 1922.
20. Ibid., July 21, 1922.
21. Inquest File of Walter Fisher, April 1926; "Widow of Slain Mokena Deputy Taken by Death," *News-Bulletin*, September 18, 1931.
22. *News-Bulletin*, March 8, 1922.
23. "Walter Fisher Gets Zahn Building," *News-Bulletin*, March 2, 1923.
24. *News-Bulletin*, March 2, 1923.
25. Ibid., June 23, 1923.
26. Ibid., August 21, 1925.
27. "The Miller-Fisher Controversy," *News-Bulletin*, July 28, 1922.
28. "Mokena Dealer Is Arrested for Bawling Out Competitor," *News-Bulletin*, July 21, 1922.
29. *News-Bulletin*, December 15, 1922.
30. Ibid., December 29, 1922.
31. Ibid., October 17, 1924.
32. "John Frisch, R.I. Employee for 39 Years, Dies," *News-Bulletin*, March 18, 1932.
33. *Joliet Evening Herald-News*, November 12, 1918.
34. *News-Bulletin*, May 25, 1923.
35. Ibid., December 21, 1923.
36. Ibid., September 1, 1924.
37. Ibid., November 7, 1924.
38. Ibid., November 27, 1925.
39. 1920 Federal Census of Village of Mokena, Frankfort Township, Will County, Illinois.
40. *News-Bulletin*, November 23, 1923.
41. Ibid., November 30, 1923.
42. "Supposed Ind. Beer Runners Pull Gun on Mokena Deputy," *News-Bulletin*, March 16, 1923.

43. "864 Bottles of Beer Seized Near Mokena," *Joliet Evening Herald-News*, March 15, 1923.

Chapter 3

44. Conversation with Dottie Ferrentino, summer 2009.
45. Ibid.
46. 1940 Federal Census of United States Penitentiary, Alcatraz Island, San Francisco County, California.
47. Conversation with Dottie Ferrentino, summer 2009.
48. Inmate Record, Illinois Department of Corrections.
49. *Lake County, Indiana Marriage Book Index 1837–1926*, Northwest Indiana Genealogical Society.

Chapter 4

50. Cook County, Illinois Death Certificate.
51. Ibid.
52. Ibid.
53. Ibid.; Inquest File of Santo Calabrese, April 1926.
54. "Fisher Killer Is Found Slain," *Chicago Herald and Examiner*, April 16, 1926.
55. "Dead Bandit Is Identified as Calahere," *Chicago Daily Journal*, April 16, 1926.

Chapter 5

56. "Bowman Plant at Mokena Will Shut Down April 1st," *News-Bulletin*, March 26, 1926.
57. "Blizzard Ties Up Country Roads," *News-Bulletin*, April 2, 1926.
58. "Harbor Police Refute Theory," *Lake County Times*, April 15, 1926.
59. Ibid.
60. Ibid.
61. "Mail Bandit Abandons Prisoner Here," *Joliet Evening Herald-News*, April 14, 1926.

62. "Harbor Police Refute Theory," *Lake County Times*, April 15, 1926.
63. "Ex–School Hero Seized as Mail Robber," *Chicago Tribune*, April 21, 1926.
64. "Harbor Police Refute Theory."
65. Ibid.
66. "Mail Bandit Abandons Prisoner Here."
67. "Harbor Police Refute Theory."

Chapter 6

68. August Maue, *History of Will County, Illinois* (n.p., 1928).
69. Inquest File of Walter Fisher, April 1926.
70. Ibid.
71. Ibid.
72. Ibid.

Chapter 7

73. Ibid.
74. Ibid.
75. Ibid.
76. "Deputy Fisher's Slayer Found Dead," *News-Bulletin*, April 15, 1926.
77. Inquest File of Walter Fisher, April 1926.
78. "Deputy Fisher's Slayer Found Dead."
79. Ibid.
80. Ibid.
81. Ibid.
82. "Deputy's 1926 Murder Part of Memorial," *Joliet Herald-News*, July 26, 1998.

Chapter 8

83. "Auto Used by Killer Found; Hunt Goes On," *Chicago Tribune*, April 15, 1926; "Lone Bandit in Mail Job, Says Driver," *Chicago Herald and Examiner*, April 15, 1926.
84. *Lake County Times*, April 14, 1926.
85. Inquest File of Walter Fisher, April 1926.

86. 1930 Federal Census of Proviso Township, Cook County, Illinois.
87. "Auto Used by Killer Found."
88. *Chicago American*, April 14, 1926.
89. Inquest File of Walter Fisher, April 1926.

Chapter 9

90. Inquest File of Santo Calabrese, April 1926.
91. Ibid.
92. *Chicago Daily News*, April 16, 1926.

Chapter 10

93. "Deputy Fisher's Slayer Found Dead," *News-Bulletin*, April 15, 1926.
94. "Calabrese Slain by Pal, Police Theory," *Chicago Daily News*, April 16, 1926.

Chapter 11

95. "Ex–School Hero Seized as Mail Robber."
96. Ibid.
97. "Recover $31,000 of Hesly's Loot in $37,000 Robbery," *Chicago Evening Post*, April 21, 1926.
98. "Trail of Boyish Theft Led Hesly to $37,000 Job," *Chicago Tribune*, April 22, 1926.
99. Cook County Illinois Birth Index, 1916–1936. Ancestry.com.

Chapter 12

100. "Admits Mail Theft, Arraigned in Indiana," *Chicago Daily News*, April 21, 1926.
101. "Hesley Whistles 'Prisoner's Song' on Way to Jail," *Lake County Times*, April 22, 1926.
102. "Hesly Identified as Slayer of Deputy Sheriff," *Chicago Tribune*, April 24, 1926.
103. Ibid.

Chapter 13

104. *Chicago Daily News*, April 15, 1926; "Sheriff Killer Identified as $37,000 Robber," *Chicago Daily Tribune*, April 18, 1926.
105. "May Link Slain Man with Theft," *Joliet Evening Herald-News*, April 16, 1926.
106. "Says Dead Man Was Not His Kidnapper," *Lake County Times*, April 16, 1926.
107. *News-Bulletin*, April 23, 1926.

Chapter 14

108. *Lake County Times*, May 26, 1926.
109. "Arraign Dan Hesly," *Lake County Times*, June 4, 1926.
110. "Hesley [*sic*] Sent Up for 25 Years," *Lake County Star*, July 6, 1926.
111. Ibid.
112. "Seeks to Indict Mail Robber on Murder Charge," *Chicago Tribune*, April 25, 1926.
113. "Judge Hunts for Jurors Himself in Murder Case," *Chicago Tribune*, April 19, 1927.
114. "25 Years for Killer; Judge Raps Verdict," *Chicago Tribune*, April 22, 1927.
115. "Mail Robber Returned for Murder Trial," *Chicago Tribune*, April 11, 1927.
116. "Doctor Tells How Hesley [*sic*] Took Auto," *Chicago Evening American*, April 21, 1927.
117. "25 Years for Killer; Judge Raps Verdict."

Chapter 15

118. Inmate File of Daniel F. Hesly, Federal Penitentiary at Alcatraz, National Archives.
119. Ibid.

Chapter 17

120. *Chicago Tribune*, August 7, 1983.
121. "Mokena Doctor, Bank President Are Married," *Chicago Heights Star*, January 18, 1952.
122. Texas Death Certificates, 1903–1952, Ancestry.com.
123. "Barney Hostert Veteran Auto Dealer, Dies Suddenly," *News-Bulletin*, December 17, 1952.
124. "John Frisch, R.I. Employee for 39 Years, Dies."
125. *News-Bulletin*, October 2, 1926.
126. Ibid., December 10, 1926.
127. Cook County Illinois Death Certificate #26214.
128. "Lucille Kaufman, 33, Dies; Formerly Lived in Mokena," *News-Bulletin*, January 24, 1952.
129. "Special Meaning in Saturday's Donation," *Joliet Herald-News*, May 7, 1999.
130. Social Security Death Index 1935–2014, Ancestry.com.
131. "Old Mokena Landmark Destroyed by Fire of Unknown Origin," *News-Bulletin*, November 8, 1929.
132. "A Tribute to Walter Fisher," *News-Bulletin*, April 15, 1926.

INDEX

G

H

I

J

K

L

M

N

O

P

R

S

T

U

V

W

Y

ABOUT THE AUTHOR

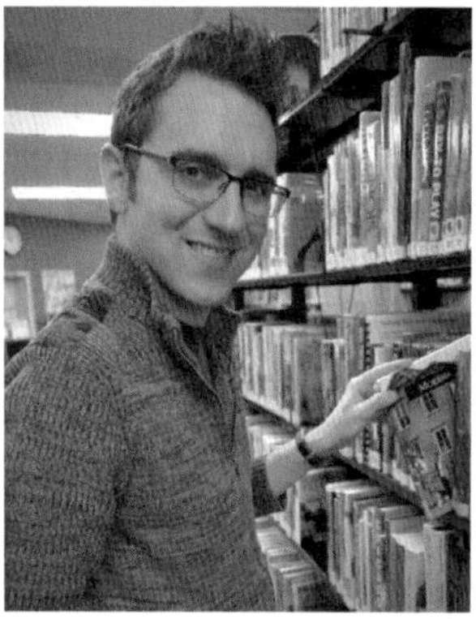

At this very second busy in a dusty archive, Matthew T. Galik is a native of Mokena and has been studying the history of the village for twenty years. He is a graduate of the University of Illinois–Chicago, having received his degree in Germanic studies, and is the author of Images of America: *Mokena* by Arcadia Publishing, as well as numerous pieces for the Will County Historical Society and the *Mokena Messenger*, where he has a column titled "Matt's Old Mokena." He has seats on both the Board of Trustees of the Mokena Community Public Library District and the Will County Historic Preservation Commission. Matt also is a Chicago tour guide, where he entertains visitors and residents alike with breezy stories of architects and gangsters.